SET IN STONE

Set in Stone

America's Embrace of the Ten Commandments

Jenna Weissman Joselit

OXFORD
UNIVERSITY PRESS

OXFORD
UNIVERSITY PRESS

Oxford University Press is a department of the University of Oxford. It furthers
the University's objective of excellence in research, scholarship, and education
by publishing worldwide. Oxford is a registered trade mark of Oxford University
Press in the UK and certain other countries.

Published in the United States of America by Oxford University Press
198 Madison Avenue, New York, NY 10016, United States of America.

Library of Congress Cataloging-in-Publication Data
Names: Joselit, Jenna Weissman, author.
Title: Set in stone : America's embrace of the Ten Commandments /
Jenna Weissman Joselit.
Description: New York : Oxford University Press, 2017. |
Includes bibliographical references and index.
Identifiers: LCCN 2016045078 | ISBN 9780190253196 (hardback : alk. paper)
Subjects: LCSH: United States—Church history. |
Ten commandments.—Miscellanea.
Classification: LCC BR517 .J67 2017 | DDC 270.0973—dc23
LC record available at https://lccn.loc.gov/2016045078

1 3 5 7 9 8 6 4 2
Printed by Sheridan Books, Inc., United States of America

For Joz

"People naturally desire to know what is expected of them, and the 10 commandments are God's answer to the question."

FRIENDS' INTELLIGENCER, 1903

"The Decalogue is entirely good stuff."

NEW YORK TIMES, 1908

"The Ten Commandments have been read for 1,500 years and they haven't stopped crime yet."

JOSEPH LEW,
President, Free-Thinkers Society of New York, 1926

CONTENTS

SET IN STONE

Introduction

No one really knows what became of the Ten Commandments. Comparable stelae, hefty stone tablets from the ancient world, are on display at the British Museum in London, the Louvre in Paris, the Pergamon in Berlin, and the Metropolitan Museum of Art in New York, but the Ten Commandments are nowhere to be found. Heralded as one of the building blocks of Western civilization, they loom large in our thoughts, but not on the ground or in the gallery. Some say the Ten Commandments vanished along with the Ten Lost Tribes; others say that the tablets, together with the Ark of the Covenant that housed them, surfaced in Ethiopia; remain hidden in a cave outside of Jerusalem; or were plundered by conquering armies. Still others question whether they actually existed at all.

No matter how hardheaded or fanciful, theories about the fate of the Ten Commandments are essentially exercises in restoration, attempts to reconcile their outsized religious, cultural, and legal presence with their glaring physical absence. Unlike other foundational texts such as the Magna Carta or the Bill of Rights, which are ours to see, the Ten Commandments do not take up space. Instead, they inhabit the confines of a book—the Bible—or live within the orbit of our moral imagination. It is little wonder, then, that theories as to their whereabouts once abounded.

Most of the time, these speculations fell wide of the mark, raising more questions than answers. In the United States, they were irrelevant. To compensate for the loss of the original stone tablets,

Americans created their own: facsimile trumped conjecture. Ever since the mid-nineteenth century, they saw to it that the Ten Commandments were just about everywhere: in houses of worship and private homes, on the street, in school, in the subway, and even on the interstate. True, the nation's citizenry may not have been able to get them quite right. Both informal and formal surveys made that clear. In 1921, for instance, the *Chicago Tribune's* "Inquiring Reporter" asked people on the street if they could recite the Ten Commandments. Most could not. Miss William Lee Randolph, an office worker, related that she had "kept track of them" until she left school. "Then I didn't have to remember them any more. I really think it is almost too much for one to memorize." Another Chicagoan, G. H. Moy, a railroad employee, had a similar experience. As a youngster, he was so familiar with the Ten Commandments that he "could recite them backwards." But with the passage of time, "I just naturally forgot them."[1]

Things were no better outside Chicago. According to a national survey conducted by the Methodist Episcopal Church in 1927, "America does not know the Ten Commandments, at least not well enough to say them." When asked to recite its provisions, many people "started out 'Thou shalt-'er,' stopped and started again, 'Thou shalt not—uh,' and on the average made no more than five attempts to give any of the Ten Commandments." The only one they were able to identify consistently and correctly had to do with adultery. Of even greater concern to the clergy of the Methodist Episcopal Church and its counterparts across the religious spectrum was the country's failure to live up to them. As far as they were concerned, Americans violated these ancient dos and don'ts right and left, honoring them more in the breach than anything else.[2]

Even so, neither ignorance nor malfeasance stopped the American people from depositing stone, paper, cardboard, stained glass, and Technicolor iterations all over the place. Drawing on every conceivable medium and opportunity, they fashioned the Ten Commandments into bookends and bookmarks, hung

illustrated versions in their parlors and schoolhouses, made multiple movies and speeches about them, and devised jaunty songs
about the perils of coveting ("Do not C-O-V-E-T, C-O-V-E-T" goes
the refrain). When not singing their praises, Americans at the grass
roots zealously planted the Ten Commandments in the landscape,
ceremoniously deposited miniaturized versions atop bar mitzvah
cakes, affixed Decalogue bumper stickers to their cars, and distributed replicas of the Ten Commandments at interfaith gatherings
to symbolize the "enduring common moral and spiritual bonds"
between Christians and Jews.[3]

Portable, lightweight, metallic versions of the biblical prescriptions dangled from female wrists, while papier-mâché equivalents
were held aloft on the steps of the United States Supreme Court.
A more substantial but equally peripatetic rendition weighing
5,280 pounds made the rounds of the southern countryside perched
astride a flatbed truck. Then again, you did not have to leave home
to encounter the tablets. Thanks to the Oriental Trading Company,
a "Ten Commandments Stand-Up" could be had for a nominal
fee. Nearly five feet tall, this cardboard Decalogue was said to be a
"sturdy decoration you'll use over and over again."[4]

Americans kept the commandments close at hand, their presence vital to, even an anchor of, their national identity. They did
not leave them alone, either. Time and again throughout the nineteenth and twentieth centuries, the nation's citizens fussed with
their physical form and, on one occasion, even went so far as to
fabricate their very own likeness of the Ten Commandments—all
with an eye toward asserting, and establishing, their claim on the
body politic. To be sure, the United States had, and continues to
have, no monopoly on the Ten Commandments. Other parts of the
world also hold it dear. In France, for example, Moses and his tablets figure prominently on church facades and within stained glass
windows. In the Holy Land, tourists and locals alike flock to Mount
Sinai. And in the global South, especially in Africa where a strong
affinity for the Old Testament coexists with pagan traditions,

some of the biblical prescriptions—the one against idolatry, for example—carry a special charge.[5]

None of these places, though, comes close to making as much of the Ten Commandments as the United States. Its attachment runs so deep that public appeals to the conscience, to do the right thing, commonly invoke them, harnessing their moral authority. In 1963, at the time of the Birmingham demonstrations, Martin Luther King Jr. brought the biblical prescriptions to bear on the civil rights movement. Every participant, from demonstrators to those working the phones, was required to sign a pledge of non-violence. "I hereby pledge myself—my person and my body—to the nonviolent movement. Therefore I will keep the following Ten Commandments," read the text. Its ten principles—among them "WALK AND TALK in the manner of love, for God is love. SEEK to perform regular service for others and for the world. FOLLOW the directions of the movement and of the caption on a demonstration"—took their shape and name, as well as their sensibility, from the ancient code.[6]

Earlier generations of Americans also kept the Ten Commandments in active circulation, insisting, along with the journalist George E. Sokolsky, that "we have no civilization, no form, no character, no distinctiveness" without them. Some went so far as to suggest that a national holiday, a "common commemoration," be held in their honor. Others, like Alabama Senator John Tyler Morgan, went further still, proposing in 1897 that American citizenship be contingent upon knowledge of the Ten Commandments. Immigrants who sought either naturalization or citizenship should be required to display a command of the Decalogue. "This is not a religious test by any means," Morgan clarified. "It is a test that goes to the constitution of society." From where he and other like-minded Americans sat, the ten divinely inspired regulations were to the modern-day citizen what the Bible had been to their colonial forebears—but better: a moral shorthand, a crystallization of scriptural precepts, as well as the

MISSISSIPPI COMMANDMENT

In the wake of the Emmett Till case, in which a young boy in Mississippi was killed for allegedly whistling at a white woman, a 1956 NAACP membership flyer drew on the symbolic power of the Ten Commandments to draw attention to the ills of racism and to recruit new members to its ranks. *Library of Congress, Prints and Photographs Division, LC-USZC4-12607* wellspring of civic order. By the late nineteenth century, the Ten Commandments had come to be an expansive American phenomenon rather than a strictly denominational one.[7]

How and why that came to pass is the subject of this book. Much has been written about the theological, philosophical, and judicial dimensions of the ancient text; attempts to reckon with Moses are nearly as numerous. Works that grapple with the tensions between church and state and with the politicization of religion are legion too. Since your bookshelves, like mine, probably sag under the accumulated weight of these interpretations, you might think that nothing can be said about the Ten Commandments that has not been said before. This book suggests otherwise. By situating these age-old rules within the context of modern America, where, ever since the mid-nineteenth century, a broad swath of the population—archaeologists and architects, building committees and set designers, politicians and savants—took their measure, my account frames the Ten Commandments as an occasion for storytelling, an exercise in history.

Far more than just a timeless, static object of contemplation, they were a barometer of their times, a catalyst of invention. Over the past century and a half, spanning the 1850s through the early 2000s—precisely the period I cover in these pages—the Ten Commandments did not just demand fidelity; they provoked discussion, even controversy. No, not theological wrangling so much as heated exchange on some of the big, juicy issues of the day: national identity, inclusion, pluralism, change. Something about the Ten Commandments—at once text and object, celestial and earthbound, Judaic and Christian—gave rise to a whole lot of "airing" and "ventilating," as one nineteenth-century observer would have it.[8]

I take my cue from that gentle characterization, envisioning this book as a series of tautly told tales in which tangible, visual expressions of the biblical prescriptions opened a can of worms— over and over again. In one instance, the Ten Commandments

This lively poster, fashioned in the wake of the Civil War, harnessed the Ten Commandments to the project of national recovery. Flanked by Lady Liberty on one side and Lady Justice on the other, the biblical code was supported by the American eagle. *Library of Congress, Prints and Photographs Division, LC-DIG-ppmsca-15858*

provoked wonder, pride, and a whiff of mystery too, when an exceedingly ancient version, or so it was claimed, turned up in central Ohio on the eve of the Civil War. In another, the presence of a Ten Commandments in the round nearly split one New York congregation asunder. In a third instance, a well-intentioned civic gesture ended up in court. Still other stories explore what happened when the Decalogue became the darling of Hollywood or, in an equally startling turn, a handmaiden to therapy. Taken on its own or, more cumulatively, as a whole, each of these narratives highlights the extent to which the Ten Commandments "pack an awful wallop," as filmmaker Cecil B. DeMille was wont to say.[9]

Having made two enormously successful motion pictures about the Ten Commandments, DeMille, perhaps more than any other figure in American history, knew full well that being walloped by the Ten Commandments was as much a physical sensation as a spiritual one. His public agreed. Whether going to the movies, taking a stroll, or staying home, Americans jumped at the chance to encounter the Ten Commandments in the flesh, so to speak. They not only kept faith with its prescriptions but also literalized them. And so do I, by organizing this book around the physical elements—stone, paper, stained glass, and film—from which earlier generations of Americans shaped the Ten Commandments. Its narrative chronicles how Americans imagined the Ten Commandments into being, positioned them above and below the earth's surface, translated them into the vernacular, rendered them common ground, and pressed them into service as a hallmark of the nation's identity. It explores the connections between the two lithic tablets and the landscape from whose depths they were excavated in the 1860s and on whose civic squares they were proudly stationed nearly a century later. It focuses on the ways in which the Ten Commandments lent themselves to dissemination, interpretation, and translation into any number of vocabularies, including the decidedly modern idiom of self-help. By offering a close look at stained-glass depictions of the Decalogue within synagogue sanctuaries throughout the country, it sheds light on American Jewry's bid for acceptance, while an analysis of movie magic and the allure of spectacular special effects shows how the Ten Commandments came to rest within the precincts of American popular culture. Thanks to DeMille's two movies about the Decalogue, the first from 1923, the second a generation later, from 1956, the biblical text now had fans as well as devotees.

If you are still wondering what became of the Ten Commandments, the following pages might just have the answer. They landed in America.

Chapter One

Species Humbug

Around 4 PM on a hot summer day in June 1860, the townsfolk of Newark, Ohio, observed one of their number, David Wyrick, acting more peculiarly than usual. The recently retired surveyor of the county of Licking, a "simpleminded, earnest man of the people, of ordinary capacity," was known far and wide for his unshakable belief that the area's array of towering Indian earthworks, its "monster stone mounds," was the handiwork of the Ten Lost Tribes. That afternoon, he was spotted making his way in and out of the stores that lined the town's main thoroughfare, brandishing an oddly shaped, polished stone, festooned with a smattering of foreign-looking words. "Almost frantic with delight," Wyrick did not know exactly what he had in hand, but from its look and feel, he strongly suspected it had to be something very old, very rare, and very precious: a holy object of the ancient Israelites, perhaps. Just a few hours earlier, the amateur archaeologist had been excavating one of the thousand-year-old Indian burial mounds so plentiful in that part of the country that it came to be known as Ohio's very own Valley of the Kings, when he happened upon the stone. No sooner was it exhumed than he ran to town "like a crazy man," recalled his young son, who often accompanied his father on his archaeological rounds.[1]

Despite their affection for Wyrick and belief in his integrity—the man's character was "abundantly and warmly attested by most respectable fellow-citizens as beyond all suspicion"—the surveyor's neighbors and several of his more professional colleagues were quick to express their skepticism about the object's authenticity. It was, they said, either the work of a practical joker or that of "some other Joe Smith," a snide reference to the founder of Mormonism, whose origins were bound up with the discovery of a buried treasure not unlike this one. Wyrick himself might have been above suspicion (though not for long), but the antiquity of his find was not. True, the earthworks were "object[s] of wonder to all tourists and of still deeper interest to all students of American antiquity," acknowledged Colonel Charles Whittlesey, a highly trained geologist of fine repute who had firsthand knowledge of them and of the "antiquity of the material universe." But the notion that they might actually contain something quite as venerable as a Hebrew relic, let alone furnish concrete proof that their architects were the Israelites of yesteryear, stretched the limits of credulity. What Wyrick took to be an object of pre-Columbian origin, counterclaimed Whittlesey, was probably no more than a fifty-year-old Masonic emblem, whose owner, in a drunken stupor, had inadvertently dropped it on the ground where "accumulations of loam and vegetation" swallowed it up, giving it the patina of old age.[2]

The geologist went on to suggest that the rheumatism from which Wyrick suffered, a disease so intense that it swelled his extremities, forcing him to retire prematurely from his official position, had gone to his head and clouded his judgment. Others, staying clear of ad hominem attacks, based their skepticism on common sense. One would think that any item that had been buried in the soil for a thousand years would be encrusted and encumbered with dirt. How, then, was it possible, wondered D. Francis Bacon in the pages of *Harper's Weekly*, that this stone emerged from its tomb "as clear and bright and slick as a new whistle?" Clearly, it was an "impudent imposture." Still others did not think much of Wyrick's discovery at all. "It tells us nothing new,—nothing of the antiquities of the country—nothing which a Scripture-read child does not know," wrote Henry Schoolcraft, one of the nation's leading geographers, in a dismissive letter to the editor of the *New York Times,* making short shrift of the amateur archaeologist's treasure.[3]

Undeterred by his critics, Wyrick continued to dig away. His steadfastness paid off a few months later, in November, when, once again, his "spade hit something hard": a small stone casket much like a treasure chest in which reposed a second lithic object of a "peculiar shape and dark color." Measuring six and seven-eighth inches long, two and seven-eighth inches wide, and one and five-eighth inches thick, its outline reportedly bore a strong resemblance to a "plain, round-topped church-window." Everything else about the stone was unusual and unfamiliar. One side contained an incised likeness, in relief, of a turban-and-tunic-clad figure of "decidedly Oriental appearance." Sporting a neatly trimmed beard and clutching an arch-shaped tablet to his breast, he was subsequently identified as a "truculent" Moses. The other side of the stone was covered from top to bottom in what appeared to be, and was later confirmed as, a variant of Hebrew script. Running every which way and into one another, the letters came together to form the text of the Ten Commandments, a slightly abridged version to be sure, and one riddled with spelling mistakes to boot, but an unmistakable version of the storied text—an "intelligent epitome"—all the same.[4]

News of Wyrick's latest discovery spread quickly, electrifying the imagination. Well before its implications were fully understood, the object generated considerable excitement, blurring the line between modern-day archaeology and old-fashioned treasure hunting, whose history in that part of the country dated to the early Republic. One eyewitness, a local dentist, reported that when Wyrick first espied the relic, "he sprung at one leap clear out the hole to the top—twelve feet—exclaiming 'I've got it!'" In the days that followed, his fellow citizens cheered him on. "Our little city has produced another wonder," exulted John Winspeace McCarty, rector of Newark's Trinity Church, who, having helped to decipher the text, had much at stake in its promotion. So too did other loyal

The 1860 discovery of a seemingly ancient version of the Ten Commandments in central Ohio excited the American imagination, furthering belief in the United States as the Promised Land. *Johnson-Humrickhouse Museum, Coshocton, OH*

sons of the Buckeye State. "If authentic," declared the *Cincinnati Daily Inquirer,* referring to the stone and its container, "they rank among the most important discoveries of the kind ever made upon this continent." The two relics furnished incontestable proof that the "sons of Jacob were walking on the soil of Ohio many centuries before the birth of Columbus," ringingly affirmed Reverend M. R. Miller of Senecaville, Ohio. Between the first of Wyrick's discoveries and this one, could anyone still harbor doubts? "Here are Hebrew letters, and words, and sentences, and law brought out from the depths of these mounds. . . . These letters are not Syriac, or Arabic, or Egyptian or Chinese. They are Hebrew, and Hebrews must have placed them where we find them."[5]

Yielding to no one in his enthusiasm, Miller insisted that the Decalogue stone was a talisman, a "veritable specimen of the very ancient Teraphim," which protected the Israelites through thick and thin, first in their native land and then on the American continent. A prized possession, it served as the "guide and palladium of the tribe." Amid such bold declarations, of which there were many, interest ran high, prompting Joseph S. Unzicker, a Cincinnati physician with a passion for local archaeology, to collect the steadily mounting number of news stories—some from as far away as New York, London, and Berlin—and to paste them into an ever-expanding scrapbook, whose pages were repurposed from the bulky body of the 1860 *United States Census of Mortality and Miscellaneous Statistics*. Now a part of the holdings of the Western Reserve Historical Society, this artifact is a bonanza of information, a testament to the nineteenth century's growing fascination with archaeology.[6]

The Decalogue stone was also photographed, sketched, traced, and cast in plaster—a "*fac-simile*," it was called—so that its likeness could be widely circulated, studied, and even made available for "autopsy," as one interested party would have it. What's more, in a rather startling departure from current scholarly protocol, Wyrick agreed to part company with his precious find long enough for the learned men of the American Ethnological Society to see for themselves what the to-do was all about. Handling the object, turning it this way and that, the organization's "savans" trained their sights on the script, whose lettering did not resemble any Hebrew characters they had previously encountered. I know my *alephs*, said one scholar, referring to the first letter of the Hebrew alphabet, and I've never seen an *aleph* like this one. With its unfamiliarly shaped *aleph* and its peculiarly formed *lamed* and *ayin*, two other letters of the Hebrew alphabet, what kind of Hebrew could this possibly be, they asked themselves, avidly discussing the finer points of epigraphy before concluding that the script that lay before them bore a sufficiently close resemblance to the Hebrew of the Bible to be classified as close kin. How, then, to account for the discrepancy between the two? Some speculated that the Hebrew on the stone might date to pre-exilic times. Others wondered if it might be the hand of a "proselyte of some long past age, imperfectly instructed in the Hebrew religion," or, better yet, the work of a "plebian, an uneducated Hebrew" perhaps?[7]

When I plowed through these accounts, awash in the technicalities of orthography and the arcana of archaeology, my eyes glazed over, but Wyrick's contemporaries could not get enough of the details. The press, from the *Ohio Farmer* and the *New York Evangelist* to the *Ladies Repository* and the *Occident and American Jewish Advocate*, obliged, filling column after column of newsprint with information about the physical dimensions and cultural import of Wyrick's finds; a steady round of public lectures fed the public's appetite for more. What accounted for the swell of interest? Getting to the bottom of "one of the greatest problems which ever bewildered the American historian" had much to do with it: Who built the stone heaps? Who were the earliest inhabitants, or "aboriginals," of the New World? Who were these "mound-builders who understood all the principal figures of geometry?" Wyrick's discovery was the latest and, for a few months at least, seemingly the most definitive development in a continuously unfolding story that dated to the early days of the Republic, when Americans first looked to the past—and the soil—to establish an ancient pedigree. Investing the mounds with great meaning, Americans of all stripes—ordinary citizens, archaeologists, ethnologists, a US president or two—believed they shone a "ray of antiquity" on the new nation. Some, quick to discount the possibility that the mound builders were Indians, the progenitors of the Cherokees and the Creeks, believed them to be an ancient race forever lost to posterity.

Other worthy candidates included Phoenicians, Romans, Leif Ericson and his band of Norsemen, as well as the Israelites, or, as one account would have it, "Jew-Tartars—mongrels in race, nationality, and religion—who probably reached our continent before the Christian era, and who built our stone mounds—*great heaps of stones*—and our tumuli—*high* places—for the same purposes for which the ancient Jews built theirs."[8]

When it came to the identity of the mound builders, "speculation had been rife," reported the *Washington Star*, understating the complexity of the situation. But no more. The Decalogue stone, and the site from whence it came, deep within a stone mound, provided a welcome measure of closure. "Does this not appear very Jewish? Does it not look very much like the act of Joshua, who wrote upon the stones a copy of the laws of Moses? See Joshua, viii, 31, 32. Does it not furnish us with strong grounds for the belief that our mound-builders were Jews—Tartar Jews, perhaps," surmised Isaac Smucker, a founding father of the town of Newark, Ohio, and, like Wyrick, a firm believer in the Ten Lost Tribes theory of origins. From his perspective, nothing more effectively shored up the antiquity of the United States than the discovery of the Ten Commandments, that age-old covenant between the Jews and their God, nestled within the bosom of an ancient burial mound. The Decalogue stone could not possibly be the handiwork of the Indians, agreed Reverend Arnold Fischel of New York's Shearith Israel congregation, holding forth at some length about the stone's provenance within the pages of the *Jewish Messenger*, a New York Jewish weekly. Even if one were to concede that the Indians had some knowledge of the "Mosaic dispensation," the way in which Moses was depicted was "so essentially different from their conceptions of manly beauty" as to render their relationship to the relic highly unlikely. The Decalogue stone could only have been the handiwork of the Jews.[9]

Years later, in 1880, when immigration from Eastern Europe was gaining momentum, flooding the New World with Jewish inhabitants of the Old, the *New York Times* had a grand old time satirizing the notion that the Jews had been the first to walk the earth in North America. In a deliciously tongue-in-cheek editorial, "Our Early Jews," the paper pointed to the recent discovery of a rock temple in Missouri in which Hebrew inscriptions were scattered about and to a recently uncovered cluster of mummies in Ohio who bore distinctively Semitic noses. These two discoveries "open a field for speculation which is all that the heart of the most enthusiastic archaeologist could desire. The finding of Hebrew inscriptions and of mummies with Hebrew noses is, of course, strong evidence that the Missouri temple and the Ohio tombs were the work of early Jews," the daily related, its unemphatic prose a form of mockery. Then again, might not the inscriptions actually "prove to be Gentile inscriptions?" True, "there is a certain plausibility in this suggestion; but the noses of the Ohio mummies cannot thus be explained away," the editorial concluded with a straight face.[10]

The gullibility of the American public was one thing, the taint of scandal quite another. The possibility that the Newark holy stones, as Wyrick's two discoveries came to be known, were pure bunk, artifacts of artifice rather than of history, perhaps even some sort of college prank, raised a lot of hackles. This too helps to explain the widespread attention they received. For every American who, like Smucker, saluted their authenticity, an equal number of his fellow citizens believed the ancient relics to be an outright hoax, a form of "delusion." Allegations of their inauthenticity thickened the air. These Ten Commandments, charged the dubious-minded, were nothing but an out-and-out scam. A work of "religious hocus-pocus," it ranked at the time as one of the "three most remarkable forgeries" in the history of archaeology. One witty critic put it even more effectively. Toying with his generation's fondness for taxonomy, he suggested that Wyrick's treasures were best classified as "Genus-Bug-Species-Hum." Not to be taken seriously, they ought to take their rightful place alongside the curiosities that populated

P. T. Barnum's American Museum, that monument to humbug. Meanwhile, doubts about Wyrick's probity steadily accumulated. Far from being a testament to the wandering Hebrews, his putative discoveries attested to the deranged psychological pleasure that a number of Americans, the retired surveyor most prominently among them, took in the "practice of deception." Perennially short of funds, and of a calculating disposition, or so it was now said, he had manufactured the relics so that he might, quite literally, cash in on them.[11]

Amid the drumbeat of criticism and what some of Wyrick's friends took to be the relentless "maltreating [that] fell upon his unhappy head," the amateur archaeologist came to regret having recovered these objects in the first place. "The Hebrew Stones, I fear, has done the evil. I wish to God someone else had found them [other than] myself," Wyrick wrote plaintively in 1863 to John Henry, the secretary of the Smithsonian Institution and a long-time supporter of North American archaeology. "Some one has been trying to hoax me." The disheartened digger might well have hoped that pointing the finger at a mysterious "someone" might clear his name and, in the process, resolve the matter of the stones' "genuineship" once and for all, but that was not to be: controversy continued to cling to their provenance, despite the ardent belief that "all the jack-knives in Christendom (even in Ohio)" couldn't possibly produce "such an outrage or piece of scholarship."[12]

That strongly worded sentence first appeared in a small pamphlet with a long-winded title: *A representation of the two stones with the characters inscribed upon them that were found by D. Wyrick during the summer of 1860. Near Newark, Ohio.* Wyrick was its author, as well as its publisher. Producing the text at his own expense, the amateur archaeologist mounted a defense of his actions. Although the text rambled and its prose was opaque and hard to follow, there was no mistaking the passion that guided Wyrick's hand. In painstaking detail, punctuated by a series of illustrations or "cuts" of the stone relics, he set the record straight on matters chronological and contextual. "It took three of us working hard from early in the morning to nearly three o'clock in the afternoon to reach the clay bed with a sufficient removal of the detritus to effect the examination desired," he wrote in one characteristic passage. "From near the undersurface, imbedded in this clay, was taken the stone box [a representation of which, as to size and shape is given on the last page of this pamphlet.]" An equally fine-grained translation of the truncated Hebrew text followed, and on its heels, a rhetorical question designed to lay to rest the possibility that Mr. Wyrick, a man of humble gifts, was capable of a hoax of this magnitude: "Would it not require a very profound scholar in Hebrew to make such an abridgement of the Hebrew Decalogue with foreign characters, as is made above?" By no stretch of the imagination did the retired surveyor of Licking County fit the bill.[13]

Wyrick's bid for acceptance did little to salvage his reputation. He died a few years later, in 1864, his name having become a byword for archaeological chicanery. Some believe that a despairing Wyrick took his own life; others believe that he succumbed to the pernicious effects of too much laudanum, which he had taken over the years to alleviate the painful symptoms of his chronic illness. One way or another, the Newark holy stones had done him in—along with the truth. Was the "simpleminded, earnest man of the people" a dupe? Had his unwavering commitment to the "Jewish theory" of American history rendered him a pawn in someone else's scheme? A number of contemporaries thought so. "We are bound to believe that in this matter he has been and is a victim, and not a 'victimizer,'" Harper's Weekly grudgingly conceded in the wake of harpooning Wyrick and his finds. But other, equally reputable, voices, among them that of Charles Whittlesey, were not quite so willing to let him off the hook. The discovery in Wyrick's workshop of a Hebrew Bible as well as a set of chisels—and, some say, bits of slate with snippets of Hebrew carving that called to mind a practice exercise—led the geologist and his fellow naysayers to insist that it was the man from Ohio, and not some other, who had fashioned the Ten Commandments in the first place.[14]

Shortly before his death, Wyrick had managed to sell his "Hebrew stones" to David M. Johnson of Coshocton, Ohio. By then, he was eager to be quit of his tainted treasures and probably in need of money too. The stones found a good home, or so it would seem at first. Johnson, reputed to be a "gentleman of taste and culture" with a keen interest in local archaeology, had outfitted the rooms of his "old family homestead" with cabinets full of fossils, minerals, shells, and a "large collection of Indian antiquities." On the strength of a recommendation from Professor Theodore Dwight, the recording secretary of the American Ethnological Society whose expertise he had solicited, the collector added Wyrick's finds to his collection. Dwight had not only pronounced them "genuine and authentic relics, notwithstanding the ridicule and suspicion thrown upon them by the skeptical," but also enjoined Johnson to "preserve them with the greatest care."[15]

Before long, the collector disregarded Dwight's advice by unloading the stones on someone else. It is not clear what changed his mind, but change his mind he did, and in short order, they were put up for sale. Hoping to benefit from the Jews' historic relationship to the Decalogue, he advertised his ancient wares in 1868 within the pages of the *Occident and American Jewish Advocate*. One of the country's leading Jewish periodicals, it had been favorably disposed toward Wyrick's discoveries from the outset, publicizing them in its pages. The sustained and positive treatment that they received, from lavishly detailed accounts of their exhumation and exceptionally close consideration of their alphabet to an equally detailed account of their significance, provided Johnson with reason to hope he might find a receptive buyer among its readers. So too did the encouragement of Rabbi Bernard Felsenthal of Chicago, the "Nestor of the American rabbinate." In a letter to Johnson, he wrote that the "stones were of high importance and will contribute much towards the solution of an interesting and difficult question in the history of Israel." Buoyed by Felsenthal's words, Johnson placed his own: "I offer for sale the Hebrew inscribed relics found in an Indian mound near Newark, Ohio," read his straightforward advertisement, without disclosing a purchase price. But there were no takers, not within the American Jewish community at any rate.[16]

Johnson kept at it, eliciting and entertaining all kinds of proposals. "My son, who is a dealer in curiosities, thinks you might place it in the window of some large store on Broadway, like that of Tiffany's with the price marked on it for passersby to look at," Nathan Brown, of the American Philological Society, wrote encouragingly in 1871. "I proposed to my son to try to sell it, but he has not the time to look after it and advertise it, which would be necessary." Eager to be helpful, and to compensate, perhaps, for his son's lack of interest, Brown went on to suggest that Johnson print up an illustrated circular "stating what is known about it and the opinions of learned men," and distribute the broadside among "every college and museum of antiquarian remains throughout the United States, and also to some institutions in Europe." Nothing came of Brown's schemes—or any other. Reluctantly, Johnson held on to the relics before donating them in the 1920s, along with thousands of other objects from his collection, to the city of Coshocton, Ohio, where, a decade later, they formed the nucleus of the Johnson-Humrickhouse Museum, a local history museum.[17]

These days, you can see for yourself what the Newark holy stones look like—and why they once generated such a hullabaloo. Now on display in a glass vitrine, as well as in the gift shop where, thanks to visitors' requests, "replicas" can be purchased for fifty-four dollars, the relics are strategically positioned within the context of the long-running debate about their authenticity rather than treated as honest-to-goodness specimens. Instead of trying to resolve whether the Newark, Ohio, objects are hoaxes or fragments of reality, the Johnson-Humrickhouse Museum has wisely chosen to interpret them as a "set of controversial stone artifacts discovered in the 1860s" that created an "immediate sensation" way back when and that continues to command attention and generate controversy among today's "archaeologists (professional and amateur), anthropologists, linguists and religious groups [who] jump into the fray armed with their field's presuppositions and data." Staying clear of that fray, the museum maintains that questions about their authenticity do not so much diminish as extend their value, providing opportunities to engage with American history. "Stone loves nothing more than story," writes literary scholar Jeffrey J. Cohen in his imaginative exploration of the relationship between the lithic and the literary in the medieval world. The same can be said of these stones, whose power resides in the stories they tell about modern America.[18]

More than a century after the Newark holy stones were first uncovered, they still make waves, especially among that broad swath of the American population with a soft spot for tall tales. Consider this: the US Bureau of Ethnology, drawing on mountains of evidence, had long ago put to rest the once-vexing identity of the mound builders, categorically proclaiming them to be native Americans. "All the mounds which have been examined and carefully are to be attributed to the indigenous tribes found inhabiting this region and their ancestors," acknowledged one of its officials in 1884, adding a few years later that the links between the Indians and the mound builders were "so numerous and well established that there should be no longer any hesitancy in accepting the theory that the two are one and the same people." Despite the bureau's assurances, you do not have to go too far afield to find contemporary Americans, among them Latter-Day Saints, who still hold on to the notion that Israelites were on the ground in pre-Columbian America. They are the ones who insist on the authenticity of Wyrick's discoveries. Still others, doggedly exploring the circumstances that gave birth to the relics, are much more interested in motivation and its psychological dimensions than in provenance and its physical properties. Inclined to doubt the historicity of Wyrick's finds, the members of this camp would like to know what made the amateur archaeologist, or those who scammed him, tick. One group, echoing its predecessors, continues vigorously to maintain that the Newark holy stones are forgeries, while another group, loudly echoing its predecessors, affirms their authenticity. Meanwhile, a latter-day generation of archaeologists and epigraphers, drawing on the latest technology, has subjected the script of the Ten Commandments to the most up-to-date of paleographic interrogations, only to come up with a range of opinions and a cast of historical characters even murkier and broader than those of a hundred years ago. As participants in this discussion exchange views over the Internet or in person at a series of symposia, talk of Samaritan mezuzahs and Sephardic merchants, of antislavery proponents and champions of polygenesis, fills the air.[19]

In 2004, Rochelle I. Altman, a specialist in linguistics, brought back into circulation a theory that had first been propounded, and quickly discounted, a century ago: that the Ten Commandments stone was indeed old, but not that old—of medieval vintage rather than of ancient origins. The property of an itinerant Jew from Spain or France, it reportedly consisted of part of a travelling set of *tefillin,* or phylacteries, which, through a series of undocumented mishaps, had gone awry and somehow ended up in Ohio. These items, Altman writes, "found their way to these sites in the United States because they were brought there, as so many family heirlooms were, by a settler from Europe searching for a new home in the new world." Phylacteries fashioned out of stone and containing the text of the Ten Commandments? How unusual! (They are generally made out of wood and leather and contain the words of the *Sh'ma,* the "Hear O' Israel" prayer.) You also have to wonder whether these *tefillin* might have sat too heavily and uncomfortably on the forehead and forearm, respectively, of their Jewish owner when he was at prayer. And how on earth did they end up within the bosom of an Indian burial mound in Ohio? Altman does not tell us: so many theories, so little evidence. Clearly, there is something about Wyrick's Ten Commandments that gives rise to fanciful, let alone wishful, thinking, even a century and a half after the fact.[20]

Since they first came to light on the eve of the Civil War, virtually everything about them, from their chronology to their composition, has been up for grabs. What renders these relics especially fascinating is not so much the various theories that attend their origins and their meanings, but what is *not* said about them. No one—then or now—batted an eye at their contents. Nary a soul wondered why, hoax or no hoax, the biblical passages that had to do with the Ten Commandments, rather than some others, were showcased in the first place. The issue simply did not come up. No one seemed to be the least bit flummoxed that the text of the Decalogue happened to materialize in Ohio one fine fall day on the eve of the Civil War. People alternately accepted or questioned the agedness of the stone's patina, the antiquity of its inscriptions, and the skill with which Moses was depicted. But no one had anything to say, one way or another, about its subject matter. It was almost as if geology had trumped reason, the stoniness of the original, biblical Ten Commandments presaging, and legitimating, the stoniness of this one. Bound together by their sturdy materiality, by their stolidity, these two Decalogues, one from the Old World and the other from the New, stood for something immutable, elemental, and durable: the fullest expression, in both substance and content, of the imperishable.

Then again, it did not take much for Wyrick's contemporaries to embrace the notion that a pre-exilic version of the Ten Commandments had washed up on their shores. By the time he announced his thrilling discovery, Americans throughout the country had taken the biblical dos and don'ts to heart, rooting them as much in the American psyche as in its landscape. Swept along by the current of enthusiasm for Moses, a lionized American hero whose transformation of a ragtag bunch of folks into a disciplined community bound by law was widely believed to parallel the nation's very own history, the Ten Commandments were heralded as an American phenomenon, through and through. The Decalogue, rhapsodized Rabbi Isaac Mayer Wise, a transplanted Ohioan and a great champion of his adopted country, as well as the architect of Reform Judaism in America, was the very "first declaration of Independence, the first proclamation of Liberty, the first and eternal blast from the trumpet of freedom." Lest anyone miss the connection between Mount Sinai and America, Wise elaborated: "Louder and mightier yet resounded that one great and powerful word of the Almighty, which was freedom! Freedom! Freedom!" What American would argue with that? Or would want to? If you were determined to establish a national identity, especially one burnished by a distinguished pedigree, there happened to be no better text on which to hang it than the Ten Commandments. In one fell swoop, it assembled the rule of law, the word of God, and the promise of singularity, joining them together in the vision of an ancient past and the prospect of a glorious future—and all under the banner of indigenousness. The Ten Commandments just happened to be the perfect foundational document.[21]

Nineteenth-century Ohio was unusually fertile in the number of antiquities it spawned. Twentieth-century California was not far behind. It too laid claim to heaps of buried treasures. But where the ancient relics recovered from the stony soil of Ohio turned out to be the handiwork of single individuals of a decidedly empirical bent, those that surfaced amid the dunes of Southern California were the collective products of Hollywood, where make-believe held sway. In that part of the country, even the practice of archaeology was affected by movie magic. Cecil B. DeMille, whose sumptuous and scrupulous reproduction of ancient Egypt in the 1923 silent film *The Ten Commandments* galvanized moviegoers, once joked about the possibility that a future generation of archaeologists might mistake the sand dunes outside of Santa Barbara for the Egyptian desert and the Pacific Ocean for the Nile River. More boast than

This broadside deftly combined the Ten Commandments with cameos of Presidents Lincoln, Washington, and Garfield, rendering its provisions an integral part of American culture. *Library of Congress, Prints and Photographs Division, LC-DIG-ppmsca-15871*

jest, his remark reflected Hollywood's belief in the adaptability, the topographical fungibility, of the California landscape. There was "scarcely a spot on the globe that cannot be duplicated within 500 miles of Los Angeles," proudly related the *Los Angeles Times*.

"You pick out a spot on the globe and [location scouts] will find it some place in southern California not more than two whoops and a holler from Hollywood Boulevard." Besides boosterism, two additional sentiments prompted DeMille's archaeological musings: pride in the set of *The Ten Commandments* and concern over its afterlife. Both weighed heavily on his mind.[22]

The splendor of the cinematic "City of the Pharoah," whose massive statuary, phalanxes of sphinxes, and towering gates stretched as far as the eye could see, more than matched, and perhaps even exceeded, that of its real-life predecessor. There is another parallel to consider: Its construction was also made possible by a huge labor force. Some five hundred carpenters, four hundred painters, and several hundred decorators working under the stylish art direction of Paul Iribe made sure the site would live up to its advance billing as the "greatest thing to come out of Hollywood." Once it outlived its usefulness, though, the entire set was dismantled. Although some of its elements—yards of timber, a couple of sphinxes—were salvaged, most of it was bulldozed and buried in the sand. There was no point in hauling the entire assemblage back to the studio; the cost would have been prohibitive. Besides, DeMille was not about to let his cherished creation fall into the hands of a rival Hollywood director.[23]

For more than sixty years, DeMille's Egypt remained underground, its long rest undisturbed by either man or the elements. Recently, as the winds shifted and the sands parted, a sphinx's nose in one spot, the tufts of a headdress in another, and the bas-relief head of a horse in a third were laid bare. Aided by El Niño, these plaster fragments and other bits of cinematic flotsam and jetsam made their way to the surface, prompting renewed interest in the site on the part of archaeologists, movie buffs, and other concerned citizens. On that basis, you could say that DeMille's prediction had come true, sort of. His Egyptian city *has* become an archaeological site. And yet, its focus does not reflect the filmmaker's particular set of concerns, but some other: with brushes in one hand and computer-generated maps in another, those in search of DeMille's "lost city" look, knowingly, for the relics of moviemaking rather than the traces of antiquity.

Unless you are inclined to think of the 1920s as ancient history, it is hard to make sense of their efforts, at least at first. You have to wonder whether it might be a postmodern experiment in the meaning of evidence. The objects of attention, after all, do not bear the weight of the ages. In fact, they do not bear much weight, period. Composed of plaster of Paris and wood, and held together by chicken wire, the set may have looked mighty authentic, all the way down to the claws on the sphinxes' paws, but absolutely nothing about it was real—or meant to endure. Way back when, film audiences might have been taken in by its larger-than-life presence, but today's archaeologists know better. No one is under any illusion that he or she has stumbled upon the Egyptian equivalent of Atlantis. How, then, to explain the commitment of considerable resources, both human and financial, to recovering the physical remains—the props—of a Hollywood movie? How to reconcile history with hokum?

The dig's proponents have a persuasive answer at the ready: even hokum deserves to have a history. "There's evidence out there in the sand of one of the biggest motion picture sets ever built," clarifies Peter Brosnan, a filmmaker who has spearheaded the recovery effort since the early 1980s and is now at work on a documentary about it. "What's out there is a piece of an era in a film that has never been matched, and never will be." It might even be the stuff of a "motion picture museum buried in the Guadalupe dunes." Brosnan has a point. No matter their age or pedigree, the artifacts associated with early Hollywood are still artifacts, "mementos of an infant industry," a part of America's cultural patrimony. The media agrees. In a reprise of its fascination with the set of *The Ten Commandments* the first time around, when members of the press seemed never to tire of tossing out statistics about the number of nails (anywhere from twenty-three thousand to twenty-five thousand pounds' worth) and the amount of wood (five hundred thousand feet) used in its construction, word of its putative recovery spread like mad, generating bold headlines ("Raiders of the Lost City") around the world.[24]

A good story on its own terms, it became an even better one when Mother Nature and Father Time entered the picture. To exhume DeMille's city before further soil erosion set in was to race against the clock. The dunes move every couple of years, exposing the set to the corrosive effects of sun, surf, and potential vandalism. And even when items are successfully recovered, they disintegrate and crumble before they have a chance to be stabilized. To complicate matters, the site of the "lost city" is now a part of a greater whole—the Guadalupe-Nipomo Dunes Complex, reportedly "one of the most ecologically significant and largest intact coastal dune ecosystems on the Earth." When, for a few months each year, the western snowy plover, an endangered species of bird, is nesting, the preserve is off-limits to everyone else. Add financial constraints to environmental ones, leaven the whole with bureaucratic snafus, and you have a dig more talked about than realized. Brosnan ruefully, and wittily, characterizes his efforts as an "epic of its own."[25]

Over the course of its fitful life, the site has yielded a couple of treasures: a handful of coins, the tip of a spear, pieces of wooden furniture, a cough syrup bottle and several tobacco tins (courtesy of the actors and workers on the set), the head of one sphinx and, since 2014, the body of another. Most of these items can be found at the Dunes Center in downtown Guadalupe, a modest institution housed in a 1910 Craftsman bungalow set off by a white picket fence. Its equally modest exhibition, "The Lost City of DeMille," which consists of those finds from the dunes that can easily fit through the door, supplemented by still photographs from *The Ten Commandments*, is a sideshow to the center's main objective of preserving the dunes and educating the public about its wildlife. Still, the display brings in visitors and with them, the possibility that, in time, the town of Guadalupe might become a tourist attraction. It is anyone's guess as to whether that will happen. In the meantime, one could envision a different future for DeMille's sand-swept city. "There's so much material out there," says Brosnan. "It might be a good place for a university to train archaeologists."[26]

You need not travel to Ohio or California, dig beneath the earth's surface, visit a museum, or attend a religious service to encounter the Ten Commandments. Ever since the late 1950s, freestanding, round-topped, granite versions, some more than six feet high, have graced the public, urban squares of virtually every state in the union, rendering the Ten Commandments a familiar sight, much less a national phenomenon. There is no mistaking these stone "monoliths," these latter-day stelae, for anything other than the Decalogue. Standing tall and confident, like sentinels, they project authority. Language enhances their commanding physical presence, as does a cluster of familiar symbols. The words of the biblical prescriptions, set forth clearly in English, cover the entire surface plane, which is further embellished by an American eagle, the Stars and Stripes, the all-seeing eye most commonly encountered on the dollar bill, a couple of six-pointed stars, a smattering of proto-Canaanite letters on two tablets, a handful of botanical flourishes, and the Christian symbol of the Chi Rho. For all its visual busyness, everything about the monument—its content and size, shapeliness and stoniness—registers immediately, legibly, and forcefully. As one of its champions proudly put it, these Ten Commandments "can be read at a considerable distance even when wet." In rain or shine, they speak of permanence. Films about the Decalogue, no matter how popular, are destined to fade away. Much the same can be said of archaeological relics; after the initial excitement of their discovery wears off, eventually they too recede from public consciousness. But stone monuments to the Ten Commandments, like the original stone tablets, were meant to last.[27]

And yet, their future does not look too bright. These days, many Americans strongly object to their presence, claiming it upsets the precarious balance between church and state and stands on its head the intentions of the Founding Fathers. Unwilling to acknowledge the civic authority of the Ten Commandments— their religious authority is another matter entirely—their detractors seek to dislodge them from the public square. These latter-day Ten Commandments would go the way of their biblical antecedents—the set that Moses smashed the first time around—and be removed from their pedestals if their opponents had their druthers. Not everyone agrees. In fact, champions of the monumentalized Ten Commandments constitute an equally mighty force, their voices as robust and their numbers just as substantial as those on the opposite side of the fence. Supporters of the monumentalized Decalogues insist they should remain where they are. Upholding rather than undermining America's heritage, their physical presence, they believe, affirms the nation's covenantal relationship with a higher power. If this segment of the population had its druthers, there would be even more of them. Neither group is willing to budge. At once a matter of constitutionality and of history, of judicial interpretation and of national identity, the stakes are too high to allow for compromise. As a result, the Ten Commandments have of late repeatedly ended up in court, their fate decided on a case-by-case basis by a panel of judges, whose ranks include the justices of the Supreme Court.[28]

To understand how the Ten Commandments became the stuff of controversy, it is best to go back to the beginning, to when the notion of a Ten Commandments monument was first circulated. Like origin stories everywhere, this one also comes in multiple versions. Some credit Cecil B. DeMille with the idea, suggesting that he alighted upon these "granite movie posters" as a way to extend the commercial reach of his 1956 film, *The Ten Commandments*, keeping it within the public's range of vision for as long as possible. Others of a decidedly less cynical cast of mind cite the contribution of Judge E. J. Ruegemer of Minnesota, who, only a few years earlier, had successfully embarked upon a campaign to post paper versions of the Ten Commandments in juvenile courts throughout the land where, he hoped, their presence might set youthful offenders on the right path. "What greater deterrent could there be to delinquency and crime than the Ten Commandments?" (J. Edgar Hoover agreed, lending his name and the imprimatur of his high office to the venture.) Still others pin the project on the Fraternal Order of Eagles, of which Judge Ruegemer was a member in good standing, an organization whose commitment to doing good was matched by its commitment to traditional American values. Boasting a quartet of US presidents—Theodore Roosevelt, Warren Harding, FDR, and Harry Truman—among its hundreds of thousands of all-white, all-male members, the national organization was established in 1898.[29]

During its early years, the order was known as much for its colorful parades as for its civic-mindedness. At annual conventions, Eagles were given to marching down Main Street dressed up as cowboys and Indians; alternatively, they sported fezes, elaborate waistcoats, and "much tinsel." In 1903, the sight of so many elaborately costumed "brothers" crowding Fifth Avenue prompted the *New York Times* to refer to "Eagles in Fine Feathers." The paper meant it literally, of course, but in the years that followed, as the fraternal order matured, that description acquired a deeper meaning. As a testament to its social conscience, the Eagles increasingly took up the banner of "humanitarian causes," advocating unemployment insurance, promoting Social Security, and eradicating juvenile delinquency. By the 1950s, the Fraternal Order of Eagles was widely acknowledged to be a "national force for good." Promoting the Ten Commandments, those "ten basic rules for right living," bolstered that claim.[30]

Somewhere along the line, these three trajectories— Hollywood savvy, judicial optimism, and grass-roots patriotism— converged. Inspired by Ruegemer's notion of keeping the Ten Commandments in circulation, DeMille made common cause with the Fraternal Order of Eagles, whose far-flung network of "aeries" or local chapters provided the perfect springboard from which to launch an ambitious promotional scheme on behalf of his film. An exchange of letters between the filmmaker and various Eagles officials, as well as a host of internal memos to DeMille from Ann del Valle, Paramount's West Coast director of publicity, and other members of the studio's publicity machine, makes clear that he actively sought out and welcomed the cooperation of the fraternal order. "If handled properly, getting people to see 'The Ten Commandments' will become an integral part of their program," del Valle assured her employer.[31]

The Eagles more than lived up to her expectations. A most willing partner, the fraternal organization raised the funds, oversaw the production process, sought out potential recipients, and generated the requisite enthusiasm among the rank and file. As one of its publications proudly put it, "Long ago on Mount Sinai . . . God gave Moses His law, the Ten Commandments on two tablets of stone. Today, God's words are again being written in stone." While the fraternal group gave God's words a big push, fashioning its tablets out of Carnelian granite—the Eagles believed this quarry most closely approximated the red granite of Mount Sinai—the filmmaker, in turn, supplied the cachet and, with the backing of the publicity department of Paramount Pictures, the star power as well. As a measure of his esteem, DeMille even saw to it that Judge Ruegemer received the gift of a bona fide artifact, a red stone tablet, from Mount Sinai itself. "I can only tell you that Mr. DeMille must think very, very highly of the project of the Fraternal Order of Eagles when he would break up one of the few sets of tablets in his personal possession in order to encourage the wonderful program you have described in your various letters," wrote Art Arthur, a member of DeMille's staff, to Judge Ruegemer in 1955.[32]

Together, Paramount Pictures and the Eagles successfully erected more than one hundred monuments, at whose dedication Charlton Heston, who played Moses in the film, or Yul Brynner, his opposite number who played Pharoah, presided. Mindful, perhaps, of the irony of his position, Brynner was given to voicing grand rhetorical statements about the significance of the Ten Commandments. "In this age of scientific development and contemporary materialistic mind, there is a greater need for spiritual guidance for all humankind," he observed characteristically in 1957 at the dedication of a Ten Commandments monument adjacent to Milwaukee's City Hall. "The need for the Ten Commandments is even greater today than it was 3000 years ago."[33]

In the aftermath of World War II, Brynner's words rang true, prompting Americans in Austin, Texas; Denver, Colorado; Wallace, Idaho; Cedar Rapids, Iowa; and Redondo Beach, California, to want a Ten Commandments monument all their own. The Fraternal Order of Eagles eagerly obliged, providing each of them with one. In Trenton, New Jersey, enthusiasm for the project ran so high that some of its citizens could barely contain themselves. Carried away by the occasion, Reverend George Chegin of St. Mary's Catholic Church, one of the guests at the dedication of Trenton's modern-day Decalogue in 1956, expressed the hope that before too long a "huge shrine honoring the Ten Commandments" might be erected in Washington, DC, where it would "tower above the Washington Monument and the Lincoln Memorial." Much to his disappointment and that of his fellow attendees who warmed to the idea of a gargantuan Ten Commandments in the nation's capital, the clergyman's vision did not pan out. Most postwar Americans contentedly made do instead with a more domesticated, smaller-scale version of a Ten Commandments monument in their own backyards.[34]

Like a nuclear bomb shelter or an early warning system, the biblical sculpture kept America out of harm's way. Of a piece with the talismanic Ten Commandments relic found in Ohio a century earlier, its modern-day counterpart, said to be more effective than the sword or the spear, the bomb or even Sputnik, possessed a similar charm: the capacity to protect Americans from their baser instincts. Then again, its functions went beyond the defensive or the prophylactic. A reminder—a lodestar—of right and wrong, a testament to "God's law," the monuments anchored the nation, setting it on its proper course. As an added dividend, they visibly distinguished the United States from other countries, such as the Soviet Union, that followed a different constellation—the red star of Communism—and whose putative godlessness stood in direct contrast with America's culture of faith.[35]

A visual proclamation of American exceptionalism, a gift to the American people, the Ten Commandments monument was hard to resist. Municipal officials, confident they enjoyed the support of their constituents, rarely turned down the Eagles' offer. Now and again, though, some did. In March 1958, Philadelphia's Art Commission rejected a Ten Commandments "slab" on the grounds that it was aesthetically unappealing. "The lettering was applied by some manufacturing process rather than cut by a sculptor or stone-cutter," complained Henri Marceau, who in his capacity as both acting chair of the commission and director of the Philadelphia Art Museum found the Eagles' version of the Ten Commandments not "artistically acceptable." Later that year, politics rather than art complicated matters. In Portland, Oregon, Julius J. Nodel, a local rabbi, took exception to his city's contemplation of the Ten Commandments. Publicly registering his dismay from the pulpit of his synagogue, Temple Beth Israel, and in the local press, he cautioned, "You don't sell the moral law through the advertising devices of a billboard display," adding that the only way for the Ten Commandments to be truly effective was to engrave them on one's heart. When Nodel was joined in his demurral by a number of liberal Protestant clergymen, the members of the local Seventh Day Adventist Church, and the Portland branch of the American Civil Liberties Union, the city decided on an alternate course of action that, it hoped, would assuage Rabbi Nodel and his allies: to situate the monolith on private property.[36]

That solution worked, quieting down a potentially volatile situation and prompting the rabbi to send a telegram to one of his rabbinic colleagues proclaiming "victory for separation [of] church and state." Isolated, short-lived, and mild-mannered episodes like this one didn't amount to anything resembling public discord. More of a gentle rebuke than a harsh rejoinder, they flickered briefly and then were gone. No extended outcry greeted a municipality's decision to erect a Ten Commandments monument. Expressions of concern lest it intrude on the landscape constitute an unnecessary and unwarranted politicization of religion, polarize the population, and violate the First Amendment were simply not heard—at least not publicly. Even Rabbi Nodel tread softly, couching his objections lyrically rather than legally.[37]

Privately, though, things looked rather different. Within the precincts of the American Civil Liberties Union (ACLU) and, most especially, those of the American Jewish Congress, the Eagles' enterprise generated grave concern, giving rise to an intense exchange of correspondence, a flurry of interoffice paperwork, and much back-channel diplomacy. Keenly alert to any sign of impending sectarianism, to any breach of the neutral public square, the ACLU joined with the American Jewish Congress, one of America's most zealous champions of an inclusive civil society, to hold the line. It took the officials of both advocacy groups a while to realize the national scope of the Eagles' campaign, but once they had, they worked energetically behind the scenes, and in concert, to persuade the fraternal order to desist. They telephoned its leaders, met with them face to face, and, lest misunderstandings accrue, sent their way a twenty-six-page legal "memorandum." Carefully crafted by the American Jewish Congress's legal staff, it detailed the reasons the monoliths were unacceptable. Drawing on both legal and instrumentalist arguments, the American Jewish Congress insisted that neither "antagonism nor indifference" to religion fueled its stance so much as the belief that both the state and religion functioned best when kept at arm's length from one another.[38]

The watchdog organization rooted its objection to the monuments in the Constitution, claiming that their placement on public property ran counter to the First Amendment, whose Establishment Clause guarded against too close a relationship between church and state. To deposit a religious symbol such as the Ten Commandments on private property was one thing, it argued. It was quite another, a thoroughly "improper" gesture, to deposit it on tax-supported, public grounds, where matters of both "constitutionality" and "propriety" militated against it. Besides, a Ten Commandments monument set a bad precedent, a "kind of first step" in the wrong direction: if the Eagles, or any other group, were to plant the Decalogue on public grounds, before you could say "God Bless America" a crèche or a crucifix would likely follow, threatening the neutrality of the public square. Everyone would be much better off were the "healthy American tradition of separation of church-state" to prevail.[39]

And that was just for starters. The monument's opponents took things even further, objecting not just to its placement but also to the very language of the Ten Commandments inscribed on its face. Departing from its customary position as guardian of the civic square, the American Jewish Congress argued that the text of the Eagles' Decalogue did not advance the cause of religion either. In a novel and arguably inspired twist, it brought to bear the little-known fact that Protestants, Catholics, and Jews each prized a slightly different version of the biblical prescriptions. Most Americans then, as now, were unaware of these differences. For the Jews, the first commandment of the lot was "I am the Lord thy God who brought you out of Egypt, the house of bondage." While not disavowing the historicity of that assertion, neither Protestants nor Catholics acknowledged its status as a commandment. For them, it figured more as a preamble. Another difference: among Protestants and Jews, the second commandment prohibited graven images; the Catholics had no such commandment. And a third: the Catholic version of the Ten Commandments contained two separate interdictions against coveting; the Protestant and Jewish versions had only one.

Such textual distinctions were nowhere in evidence on the Eagles monument. True, a quick glance would not have turned up anything untoward: all of the "Thou shalts" and "Thou shalt nots" seemed to be present and accounted for. But a more sustained look revealed a text that contained elements drawn from the Jewish, Protestant, and Catholic formulations. In an attempt to reconcile the three variant readings, to arrive at a version that would sit well with Protestants and Catholics, as well as with the Jews, the ancient biblical injunctions had been "rearranged" by a trio of latter-day Americans from the nation's heartland. Working together, across religious lines, a representative from each of the Protestant, Catholic, and Jewish communities of Minnesota, where the Eagles had its headquarters, had fashioned a Ten Commandments that had something for everyone. "I am the Lord thy God" was there, the prohibition against graven images was there, and the two proscriptions against coveting were there, too. The only thing missing were the numbers that identified each commandment. It was not that the Eagles had run out of room. A deliberate omission, the absence of Roman numerals, or any other kind of numbering system for that matter, avoided the mathematical probability that the Eagles' version of the Ten Commandments more closely approximated nine or eleven, depending on who was doing the counting.[40]

A nimble strategy, you might think. What could the American Jewish Congress and the ACLU possibly find wrong with it? What was so objectionable in the revamped text that it called to mind the triple threat of "bad theology, bad pedagogy, and bad law"? Was the Jewish organization troubled by the fact that an interfaith committee of three sitting in Minnesota in the 1950s had reassembled the words of God? Did the new version strike its legal staff as a demonstration of hubris perhaps, or, worse still, as an exercise in blasphemy? Probably not. What fueled the American Jewish Congress's dismay was its belief that reworking the text was less a demonstration of goodwill and brotherhood or an expression of fidelity to a common set of biblical values than a sleight of hand,

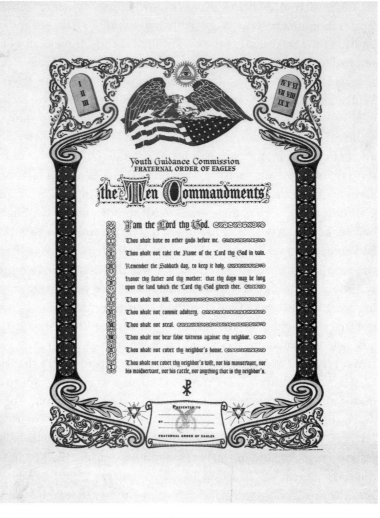

The Fraternal Order of Eagles distributed thousands of copies of this paper certificate bearing the Ten Commandments, laying the groundwork for their subsequent reappearance in the form of stone monuments. *Library of Congress, Prints and Photographs Division, LC-DIG-ppmsca-15861*

a strategic move designed to render the biblical commandments nonsectarian and hence noncontroversial, the better to station them on public property without causing a stir. That exercise came at too great a cost—to religion.[41]

Defining the Ten Commandments as a nonsectarian document "belie[d] their intrinsic character" as a theological statement, distorting rather than advancing the cause of religion. In the American Jewish Congress's fighting words: "To treat the Ten Commandments as an adjunct of sociology, community relations or other of the secular sciences would be to denigrate their authentic purpose, to divest them of their transcendental meaning." And more: "To reduce the Ten Commandments to the level of mere moral instruction would be to sever them from their root and core. The Ten Commandments have never been regarded as a mere copy book of maxims or [a] handbook for practical conduct." Put simply, to characterize the Decalogue monuments as nonsectarian was an act of "camouflage," of putting one over on the American people.[42]

Despite the American Jewish Congress's efforts to speak in the name of the entire body politic, to make clear that it was acting in good faith, in the full-throttled voice of America's citizens and not in the aggrieved tones of an embattled minority, opposition to the Ten Commandments monuments was largely understood to be a Jewish issue. America's Catholics were inclined to welcome them and Protestants apt to temporize, but the Jews were "unanimous in their opposition," declared Rabbi Albert Vorspan, director of the Reform movement's Commission on Social Action, a perspective seconded by Joseph Minsky of Chicago, the Midwest director of the American Jewish Congress. "No other group" is prepared to challenge the Eagles, he glumly observed as early as 1957.[43]

It should come as no surprise, then, to learn that Donald Hayne, a Paramount Studios executive who worked in tandem with the Eagles to promote the Ten Commandments campaign, singled out the Jews as the ones most likely to derail their project. When it came to his attention that not only had the American Jewish Congress taken on the Eagles but also a prominent Minneapolis rabbi, Albert Minda, had publicly retracted an earlier commitment to the venture, Hayne sprang into action. He alerted his boss. "Jewish organizations and rabbis are fighting the Eagles' efforts to enshrine plaques of the Ten Commandments in public schools and other public places," he duly informed DeMille, strategically comparing their opposition to the furor that had greeted *King of Kings*, the filmmaker's account of the life and death of Jesus, thirty years earlier, in 1927.[44]

Back then, even as influential interwar critics such as Mordaunt Hall of the *New York Times* hailed the motion picture for the excellence of its acting and its attention to detail, even predicting that *King of Kings* would become a "film that begets reverence," America's Jews did not quite see things that way. Where Christian America showered the film with hosannas, Jewish America pummeled it with brickbats. Generating a public relations crisis of the first order, its members decried the movie as "this Oberammergau of Hollywood, [a] vicious, defiling and wanton attempt to revive the myth of the Christ-killing Jew," and called for it to be pulled from circulation or, at the very least, actively boycotted by their cinema-going coreligionists. Ultimately, after much to-ing and fro-ing between the Anti-Defamation League and DeMille's representatives, some of the film's more inflammatory scenes and intertitles were dropped and a foreword added in which the Jews were "exculpated" for the death of Christ. American Jewry may have been mollified by these gestures of goodwill, but DeMille never fully got over the community's public assault on his good name. It remained a real sore point.[45]

Hayne knew that, of course. Invoking the specter of the *King of Kings* was his way of raising the stakes, of underscoring the extent to which American Jewry's opposition to the Ten Commandments monolith campaign constituted a "serious and very delicate problem," which needed to be handled diplomatically and thoroughly "overcome" this time around, lest the planting of the Ten Commandments run aground. Perhaps a number of American Jews could be found who, "sympathetic" to the Eagles project, might "approach" their coreligionists and urge them to relax their "adamant" position, Hayne suggested. Failing that, perhaps the Jews might come to realize they were in the minority and rethink their opposition. Let's hope, said Hayne, that the "Jewish group may not choose to stand out against the majority opinion of the other groups." And if that did not work, maybe the Eagles could secure "solid and objective documentation" to discount American Jewry's concerns, or, as the public relations executive colloquially put it, the "proof of the pudding is in the eating." Could the Eagles rustle up sufficient evidence to prove that American Jews had nothing to fear from a monument to the Ten Commandments, that their anxiety was "groundless"?[46]

Like DeMille, the Fraternal Order of Eagles was equally disturbed by the Jewish community's reluctance to support its initiative. Had not the organization extended itself, possibly even at the risk of antagonizing its own constituents, by promoting a consensual account of the ancient text? "May I suggest that you who live in a Protestant nation, read your Bible, by which I mean a Protestant version," complained one Eagle from Seattle in 1957, taking great exception to the monument's inscriptions, which, he insisted, were not "as God set them forth." Protesting the attempt "to foist this ungodly version on unthinking brothers," he called for an immediate apology. None was forthcoming. Instead, the disapproving brother was duly informed that "after consultation over a period of years with the clergy of many denominations, a universally acceptable translation of the Ten Commandments from the Old Testament was adopted for use on the monolith." Imagine, then, the organization's consternation upon learning that its motivations were suspect and that the text it had so carefully and amicably crafted did not pass muster.[47]

Its dismay notwithstanding, nothing stopped the Eagles from forging ahead and planting as many Ten Commandments mono- liths as they possibly could. Despite the vexing issues raised by— and troubling—the American Jewish Congress and the ACLU, the fraternal group continued to believe that it had "perfected a truly non-sectarian version of the Commandments," and that its project was thoroughly "non-denominational" and wholly appropriate. There was no convincing them otherwise. What, then, did the two civil liberties groups do in response? Having failed to deflect the Eagles, they folded their tents and walked away. Instead of taking them publicly to task—or to court—the American Jewish Congress and the ACLU decided not to pursue the matter.[48]

It is not that they lacked interest or the resources to challenge the Ten Commandments monoliths. Other church–state issues, from school prayer and Bible readings to the posting of paper ver- sions of the Ten Commandments in classrooms, left them "agog," as one newspaper would have it, prompting considerable institutional concern, even judicial action. When, early in 1957, the American Legion of Long Island launched what it called an "all-out drive" to install its very own, numberless version of the Ten Commandments in schools across the region—the so-called Public School Ten Commandments—claiming this document was no different from the Pledge of Allegiance, the American Jewish Congress was at the ready, quick to throw down the gauntlet of constitutionality. When, two years later, a local school board in Savannah, Georgia, made known its intentions to post the Ten Commandments in its classrooms so that its young citizens would be "reminded of what is right," the American Jewish Congress was immediately on the case. Closely monitoring the situation and working quietly behind the scenes, it advised the Savannah Jewish Council on how to mount an effective legal challenge.[49]

Why, then, was the Fraternal Order of Eagles given a pass? Any number of explanations come to mind. For one thing, the inability of either the American Jewish Congress or the ACLU to whip up sufficient external support tempered the drive for a protracted fight. Time and time again, reports from the field gave voice to both disappointment and frustration at the lukewarm response of the general public. "Unfortunately, we have not been able to get off the ground in having any type of community protest," acknowledged Joseph Minsky, the American Jewish Congress's representative in Chicago, in what soon became a standard refrain. "Last week, I did some calling through the area but was unable to achieve any real enthusiasm" for our efforts. Without it, there was no point in going forward.[50]

The decision to hold back, to stay the hand of protest, can also be explained by less sociological and more theoretical concerns: those that reside in the distinction between a public sculpture and a classroom, between passive and active forms of engagement, between looking and doing. In the manner of public statuary everywhere, the Ten Commandments qua monument welcomed attention but did not insist upon, let alone compel, it. In school, on the other hand, where the iron fist of discipline reigned supreme, looking the other way was no option. Impressionable youngsters were apt to mistake God's rules for the rules of the classroom.

Lastly, and perhaps most significantly, the decision to walk away from this fight was a matter of comity. Rocking the boat was in no one's best interest, certainly not in the best interest of America's Jews, who, after all, were eager to fit in, not stand apart. At the time, and well into the 1960s, the Ten Commandments monoliths were understood by most Americans as affirmations of the commonweal. The prospect that this salute to the biblical precepts might possibly be construed as a set of shackles rather than a common bond would have been unthinkable—even among the most resolute champions of the First Amendment. Enlarging the parameters of community, the Ten Commandments were touted as the stuff of common ground and consensus, or what would increasingly become known as the "Judeo-Christian tradition."

Although at no time did the Eagles, or, for that matter, DeMille and his people, make explicit use of that phrase, the notion that Judaism and Christianity might find "common purpose" and a common core without "submerging [their] distinctive teachings" was already in the air and had been ever since the war. At first, talk of both the "Hebrew-Christian tradition" and the "Judeo-Christian tradition," terms that were used interchangeably, was the stock-in-trade of Catholic, Protestant, and Jewish theologians and scholars who, beginning in the late 1930s, gathered together for study at the Jewish Theological Seminary in New York on a Tuesday, the one day of the week that clergy had available for extra-ecclesiastical pursuits. Tuesdays at the Seminary were full, consisting of two morning lectures and discussions, followed by lunch and then another round of intellectual activity. Conversations typically covered a lot of ground, from a comparative look at Saint Augustine and Rabbi Akiba to an inquiry into the "religious background of American constitutional democracy." For many of the participants, the high point of the day was not to be found in the classroom or at the lectern but around the table. "There was clearly great significance in the breaking of bread together and the opportunity for informal conversation with other registrants who were to be met nowhere else," recalled Jessica Feingold, who, in her capacity as director of Intergroup Activities at the Seminary, orchestrated the gatherings.[51]

Little by little, references to the "Judeo-Christian tradition," a "byproduct" of the Tuesday elite discussions, began to make their way into common parlance. Picked up by politicians, expounded upon by sociologists, and publicly sanctioned by such leading Protestant theologians of postwar America as Reinhold Niebuhr and Paul Tillich, the term became both respectable and normative: a collective acknowledgment of the partnership between Judaism and Christianity. By the early 1950s, historian Mark Silk tells us, "good Americans were supposed to be, in some sense, committed Judeo-Christians. It was a recent addition to the national creed." Monuments to the Ten Commandments furthered the nation's newfound Judeo-Christian credo by visualizing it. They rendered tangible postwar America's vision of interreligious cooperation, placing its commitment to "empathy and sympathy" in plain sight—for everyone to see.[52]

That the Ten Commandments bore an earthly, as well as a divine, seal of approval boosted their popularity even as it curbed an appetite for public dissent. President Harry Truman was a big fan. The recipient of an illuminated print of the Ten Commandments, a present from the Minnesota branch of the Fraternal Order of Eagles that he publicly acknowledged—and with a widely distributed, accompanying photograph, no less— the postwar president had high praise for the group's campaign to promote the Ten Commandments, which accorded perfectly with his own worldview. By his lights, the only guidelines Americans needed to lead an ethical life were the Ten Commandments and the Sermon on the Mount; everything else was extraneous. More to the point, Truman was quoted as saying that the government of the United States was "patterned to some extent from the law presented to Moses on Mount Sinai." Any American who read of the president's response might easily deduce that the granite Ten Commandments monuments erected from coast to coast carried his blessing.[53]

For half a century, these monuments, like other public sculptures, weathered the passage of time. Dedicated with great fanfare, they settled quietly into place, becoming as much a part of the civic square as its lampposts and signage—which is to say, unremarkable. Over the years, birds perched atop their rounded edges, leaving their mark; cracks appeared in the granite and were not repaired; the surrounding foliage grew denser, the inscription grew fainter, and passersby strolled past without giving the Ten Commandments so much as a second look. On several different occasions over the years, while teaching a seminar on the Ten Commandments at Princeton University, I brought groups of students to Trenton to visit its biblical monolith. Time and again, they walked right by without acknowledging its presence. Obscured by a cluster of trees and looking the worse for wear— anything but monumental—the granite pillar failed to make itself known. After several minutes of our walking to and fro on the grounds of the Trenton State Courthouse, I would have to point out the monument's location. Sheepishly, we then walked toward it, only to stand silently before its diminished aura. To a person, the students were taken aback, hard-pressed to reconcile the tar- nished reality of this Ten Commandments monolith with the high- minded rhetoric that attended its establishment and, more to the point, with the fiercely worded challenges to its legitimacy. In the way of undergraduates everywhere, quick to boil things down to their essence, they had only one question: why all the fuss? Each time, I sputtered something about the power of symbols, how what mattered was not so much what they looked like as what they stood for, but whatever I mustered by way of a response invariably came up short.

It fell to another passerby to make clear what was at stake. Day in and day out, Thomas Van Orden, an unemployed, homeless law- yer in Austin, Texas, would make his way to the Texas State Law Library, where he not only found shelter from the elements but also kept himself busy, researching the finer points of the law. To reach his destination, which was located just a stone's throw away from the Texas state capitol, Van Orden had first to pass a gauntlet of seventeen monuments, each of which was dedicated at differ- ent points in time and executed by different pairs of hands. One monument memorialized the state's Civil War dead, another put "Texas Pioneer Women" on a pedestal, while a third, a gift to the "people and youth of Texas" from the Fraternal Order of Eagles of Texas, saluted the Ten Commandments. Little bound them together other than the grass on which they stood and a touch of "fortuity" or happenstance. All the same, if you were so inclined, you could conceivably liken the entire assemblage to an outdoor sculpture garden. Van Orden was not so inclined. Where others saw a constellation of innocuous stone sculptures, he saw a red flag. In 2002, this most unlikely of plaintiffs who lived in a tent and subsisted on food stamps sought, and won, an injunction to have the Ten Commandments monolith removed from the precincts of the Texas state capitol on the grounds that it violated the First Amendment. "I don't have anything against religion," the former criminal defense lawyer told Jan Jarboe Russell, a reporter for *Texas Monthly*. "I'm not a radical. I just think government can't take sides when it comes to religion." After years of snaking its way through the lower courts, during which Van Orden's brief was joined by the American Jewish Congress, the Americans for Religious Liberty, and People for the American Way, among many others, *Van Orden v. Perry* came before the United States Supreme Court in 2005, where it was soon to make waves. "Even a guy who sleeps under a bush has a duty and a right to fight for his constitutional rights and make history," the plaintiff declared. "It's a great country, isn't it?"[54]

The constitutionality of the Texas Ten Commandments was yoked to that of another contemporaneous display: gold-framed paper copies of the King James Version of the Decalogue that had been installed in the corridors of two Kentucky county courthouses as late as 1999. When the local branch of the ACLU got wind of this development and sued, county officials responded by augmenting the Ten Commandments with the text of the Mayflower Compact and the motto "In God We Trust," two other foundational texts with religious themes, hoping that the Ten Commandments would now be in good, and unassailable, company. That strategy did not work. The district court entered a preliminary injunction ordering the display to be taken down immediately. The Kentucky officials stood their ground. Instead of removing the installation, they put up another one, their third, adding the Magna Carta, the words of the "Star-Spangled Banner," and an image of Lady Justice to the mix. Once again, the county believed that a broad-based installation would pass muster where a stand-alone Ten Commandments would not. And once again, it was proved wrong. The ACLU took the Kentucky counties to court, where, eventually, *McCreary County v. American Civil Liberties Union of Kentucky* ended up before the nation's highest tribunal.

"The profile of the Ten Commandments, it seems, has rarely been higher, or their ability to attract lawsuits greater," observed Linda Greenhouse of the *New York Times*, adding that the two cases before the Supreme Court were of great moment when it came to pinpointing the appropriate constitutional boundaries between church and state. True enough. But the law was not the only thing on trial. So too was another form of precedent: the weight of the past. The role of the Ten Commandments in the shaping of America's national character—a role that was at once historic and ongoing—was also in the dock. The divine sayings had become increasingly associated with conflict and debate, inflaming rather than stabilizing the public square. In twenty-first-century America, they symbolized a looming cultural divide between those eager to blur the line between church and state and those just as eager to keep it intact, between those who promoted religion everywhere and those who preferred to have it privatized.[55]

Then again, the legal standing of the Ten Commandments was not only a referendum on the role of religion in contemporary America. It was also a referendum on history, on the nation's under-standing of its past, on the degree to which religion—or, more to the point, biblical values and ideals—defined American identity. Mingling past and present, current concerns about the direction in which the country was headed with an awareness of what had gone before, the Ten Commandments cases went to the very heart of how contemporary America saw itself: pursuing its own course or following in the footsteps of history. Notionally about America's cultural heritage, as well as its legal system, they "are about more than a Ten Commandments monument in front of a state capi-tol or hanging on the wall of a courthouse," acknowledged one contemporary observer. "They are about the kind of America we are going to have."[56]

With so much at stake, feelings ran especially high on the bench. If the published remarks of the justices are any indication, they shared Greenhouse's sense of occasion. Justice Antonin Scalia, who voted to retain the Ten Commandments in stone and in paper, declared rather scathingly that those of his colleagues who sought their removal were angling to "sandblast the Ten Commandments from the public square" and to "abandon our heritage in favor of unprincipled expressions of personal preference." Those on the receiving end of his tongue-lashing responded in kind. "It is true that many Americans find the Ten Commandments in accord with their personal beliefs," observed Justice Sandra Day O'Connor. "But we do not count heads before enforcing the First Amendment."[57]

Ultimately, the court decided in favor of one display and against the other, "immunizing the first from constitutional challenge," while barring the second. Both decisions pivoted on the issue of context. "Our cases, Janus-like, point in two directions," acknowledged Chief Justice William Rehnquist. "One face looks toward the strong role played by religion and religious traditions throughout our Nation's history. . . . The other face looks toward the principle that governmental intervention in religious matters can itself endanger religious freedom." Tiptoeing between history and the law, the Rehnquist Court, in a five-to-four decision, ruled that the Texas Ten Commandments did not violate the Establishment Clause. "A passive monument" did not constitute an endorsement of religion so much as a recognition of the role that religion had played in American life," concluded a plurality of the justices, who, in rendering their decision, took both the form and the pedigree, the historical context, of the Eagles' Ten Commandments into account. For them, the pull of history was too strong to be resisted, much less discounted. As the court put it, the "Ten Commandments have an undeniable historical meaning."[58]

At the same time, the justices ruled, also in a split decision, that the Kentucky versions, cloaking their religious intentions in a "transparent claim to secularity," clearly "ran afoul" of the Establishment Clause. There was no mistaking the counties' motivation, explained Justice Souter, who wrote the majority opinion. When, at the dedication of the Ten Commandments display in Pulaski County, its county executive was accompanied by his pastor, any "reasonable observer could only think that the Counties meant to emphasize and celebrate the Commandments' religious message." For other members of the bench, such as Justice Stephen Breyer, the current cultural context—polyglot America—was equally key. "A more contemporary state effort to focus attention upon a religious text is certainly likely to prove divisive in a way that this longstanding, pre-existing monument had not," he related, distinguishing between the Texas Ten Commandments and the Kentucky version, between America of the 1960s and its twenty-first-century counterpart.[59]

Such fine-bore distinctions were lost on the grass roots, which preferred a definitive, unequivocal ruling—"yea" or "nay"—to one that trafficked in the niceties of history and sociology. As the *Wall Street Journal* baldly put it in the wake of the court's decision: "What gives?" Van Orden, for his part, declared himself "not happy" by the judicial outcome. He was not the only one. James Dobson, the founder of Focus on the Family Action, an influential conservative Christian lobbying group, took the court to task for "failing to decide whether it will stand up for religion and freedom of expression or if it will allow liberal interests to banish God from the public sphere." The legal community was none too happy either. It too would have preferred a clear-cut ruling instead of the kind of dueling perspectives that opened the floodgates of analysis, generating reams of commentary in legal periodicals that ran the gamut from the *Texas Review of Law & Politics* to the *Harvard Journal of Law & Public Policy*. Muddying the waters, the situation, as legal expert Noah Feldman put it, was a "mess."[60]

Among those reeling from the Supreme Court's rulings was Judge Roy Moore, a former chief justice of the Alabama State Supreme Court, who pronounced them a "devastating blow to Christianity in this country." A man of faith as well as an astute politician, he had defied long-standing legal precedent, much less a federal court order, just a few years earlier, in 2001, by installing a 5,280-pound rendition of the Ten Commandments inside the grand rotunda of the Alabama State Courthouse, where it could not be missed. May it "mark the restoration of the moral foundation of law to our people," Moore declared at the sculpture's ceremonial unveiling, all too mindful of the controversy he was about to ignite and itching for a fight. Scratches and scuff marks on the building's marble floor attest to the ensuing kerfuffle. The "Ten Commandments Judge" would not let his monument go. It took a vote of his colleagues on the bench and a team of workers, straining mightily, to dislodge "Roy's Rock" from its position, moving it out of sight and into storage. The granite monument was not the only thing removed from the Alabama State Courthouse. After the judge refused to budge from his ideological position, he too was removed.[61]

Despite the loss of both status and sculpture, Roy Moore was not about to go quietly. Resolved to redeem his two-ton sculpture from disgrace, he arranged for it to be placed atop a flatbed truck and sent on its way, making the rounds of the Southern countryside on a "Faith and Freedom Tour." As the displaced Decalogue rolled into one small town after another, local residents lined the streets to give it a warm welcome, respectfully forming a queue and patiently awaiting their turn to take a snapshot of themselves and their kinfolk standing next to it. Some ran their hands lovingly over its surface; others kneeled before it. At once a shrine and matter out of place, the wandering Ten Commandments and the veneration with which it was greeted brought to mind the biblical Ark of the Covenant, which, housing the original Ten Commandments (in both their fragmented and intact states), accompanied the

Israelites on their peregrinations through the desert. Anyone who knew his or her Bible would be struck by the parallels between this latter-day tabernacle and its biblical antecedent. Moore's decision, then, to take the Ten Commandments on the road, "to bring [them] into the light of day," was inspired. Not just a harebrained scheme or a defiant political gesture, it spoke to the imprint of the Bible on the American imagination, to the conflation between the ancient Israelites and the American people, and to the ongoing luster of the divine presence.[62]

For more than a century, the Ten Commandments had been planted in and exhumed from the soil, quarried from local sources, deposited in the public square, and widely circulated. Called into being by the artistry of woodcarvers, the skill of stonemasons, and the religious convictions of magistrates, as well as by the goodwill of lodge members and the long arm of Hollywood, the Ten Commandments were heralded by a wide swath of Americans who went to great, and often inventive, lengths to express their admiration for—and need of—them. So deep ran their investment in the ancient text that they believed in its organic connection to the American landscape and its people. Some made good on that belief by fabricating a version of the Decalogue and hailing it an ancient relic, others by treating movie props from *The Ten Commandments* as if they were the real deal, and still others by fashioning monuments as if they were props on the national stage. Though made in America and by all-too-human hands, these Ten Commandments bestowed a sense of completeness on their followers, who, in turn, endowed the biblical code with the gift of resonance. Placing the Ten Commandments before their eyes and well within reach, Americans affirmed their value as words to live by.

Chapter Two

The Ultimate To-Do List

Assemblyman Charles Walters, a Populist politician from Kansas, was in a bit of a tizzy. If the behavior of his fellow Americans was any indication, the Ten Commandments no longer had the power to command. Amid the blandishments of modernity, they were fast losing ground, prompting the male population in particular to do "those things they ought not to do"—and with impunity. "The men of the present generation," Walters observed in 1897, "have become doubters and scoffers; [they] have strayed from the religion of their fathers . . . [and] wantonly violate the law given to the world from Mount Sinai." Not one to sit on his hands, the politician was determined to restore the commandments to their rightful place. But how? His counterparts in New York might invoke the biblical covenant at a rally, seeking to rouse a rowdy crowd to action: "Three cheers for the Ten Commandments," they would say. "Let's hear it for the Ten Commandments." Back in Kansas, though, sloganeering was not enough. The situation called for stronger measures: a bill rather than a bullhorn.[1]

Seeking to put teeth back into the Ten Commandments, Walters proposed a piece of far-reaching legislation that would incorporate each commandment into Kansas law, endowing it with "statutory force." Were he to prevail, the fifth commandment, for example, would receive a new lease on life as "Section 5" of the Kansas legal code, and the seventh commandment would henceforth be known as "Section 7." More to the point, perhaps, those guilty of violating Sections 5 and 7, as well as Sections 1 through 4 and 6, 8, 9, and 10, would have to answer to law enforcement personnel, as well as to God or their pastor. If a resident of Kansas City was found guilty of treating his parents badly, he could be fined $500 and face the prospect of six months in jail. If a resident of Topeka committed adultery, his future did not look at all bright: he might have to spend the rest of his days in the state penitentiary.[2]

Something new was in the air, and it was not just the harshness of the penalties that awaited those Kansans who gave the Ten Commandments short shrift. Nor was it the way in which Walters's proposition, soon known as the "Decalogue Bill," formally acknowledged the power of the Ten Commandments. What rendered his proposition so striking, so novel, was its direct and unmediated importation of the biblical covenant into America's judicial system. Few Americans at the time were likely to disagree about the impact of the Ten Commandments on American jurisprudence. One way or another, whether construed as divine law, natural law, or common law, the biblical construct made itself felt. The Ten Commandments informed America's ideas of right and wrong. Their spirit hovered over legislation that outlawed murder and theft, mandated Sabbath observance, and checked the human impulse to rail at God. But, at nearly every turn, the presence of the Ten Commandments was more a matter of high-minded rhetoric and allusion than of formal procedure. Had Walters carefully combed through extant case law, he would have found few, if any, instances in which it rested explicitly on the Decalogue. Not that this would have stayed his hand. The legislator had in mind to reverse the course of modern American legal history by expressly codifying the Ten Commandments as American jurisprudence. If he had his way, the spirit and the letter of the law would be one.[3]

Walters went too far. Although a handful of Kansans at the grass roots applauded his efforts, even thanking God for the "one man that was willing to stand by the old and tried," Walters's proposal received quite a shellacking from his legislative colleagues. It did not stand the faintest chance of passing, not even on the

third try. Some called the bill absurd, others "daffy," and still others labeled it casuistic. Everyone wished it would go away. Was it
fear of God that motivated their opposition? Or concern, perhaps,
for the First Amendment? No, nothing quite as lofty as that. What
fueled the resistance of Walters's comrades was the prospect of
looking rather silly. No Kansas politician wanted to be put in the
position of having to confirm the wisdom of Moses or, worse still,
of having to vote "yea" or "nay" on the Ten Commandments. It was
far better to give Walters's proposal a wide berth than to appear
foolish. Outside the corridors of power, especially among the press,
the well-intentioned assemblyman, the father of four, did not fare
much better either. The fifth estate pilloried him. Within the pages
of diverse newspapers such as the *Topeka State Journal* and the *New-
York Daily Tribune,* he figured as an object of derision. Walters has
the "courage of his absurdities," charged one daily, while another
facetiously suggested that "some Kansas sculptor should do for
him what Michael Angelo did for Moses, and set him up in enduring bronze in the Capitol at Topeka." A third publication wryly
observed that Walters's initiative underscored the "fertility of the
legislative mind."[4]

To no one's surprise save his, nothing came of the monument
or the legislation. More of a footnote than a phenomenon, the
"Decalogue Bill" remained a flash in the pan, yet another in a very
long series of curiosities in which American history—and this
book—delights. Even so, it hinted at a collective change of heart
toward the Ten Commandments, a subtle dethroning that would
generate increasingly insistent questions about their role in modern society as the nineteenth century gave way to the twentieth.
"What do we, satisfied Americans, know or care about those old,
unevoluted Ten Commandments—especially we of the divorce
court what know or care of the outdated Seventh Commandment?"
said one of their number, referring, of course, to the interdiction
against adultery. Said another satisfied American, a touch categorically, "The Ten Commandments are as inadequate a moral code

If legislator Charles Walters of Kansas had had his way, violating the biblical interdiction against blasphemy would have become a civic offense in late
nineteenth-century America. *Warshaw Collection of Business Americana—
Religion, Archives Center, National Museum of American History, Smithsonian
Institution*

today as camels are for transportation." Were these age-old precepts still relevant to the lives of modern-day Americans? Could
they continue to believe in their authoritativeness? At a time when
"old notions of right and wrong are scouted in some quarters as
old wives' tales," could the all-encompassing moral authority of
the Ten Commandments still be assumed? Or, as Felix Adler, the
founder of the progressive Ethical Culture movement, put it several years before the "Decalogue Bill" was even a gleam in Walters's
eye, "When there are so many pressing problems that challenge
our attention," should we even be discussing this ancient code?[5]

Though he posed a tough question, Adler was by no means prepared to ditch the Ten Commandments, not quite yet. In a well-
attended lecture at Carnegie Hall in 1895, he sought to make a
case for them, insisting they were not in the least bit "superfluous,"
especially when seen in the light of modern-day concerns. The

commandment against theft "has not become antiquated in these days of trusts and railway corporations," he argued, referring to mounting public concern over the monopolization of capital, nor had the commandment mandating a day of rest become obsolete when calls from the laboring classes for a shorter workweek had grown louder and more insistent. The Ten Commandments still had much to offer, especially for the younger members of society. "The best thing that can happen to them," Adler declared, "is to grow up from earliest infancy under the shadow and in the awe of the Great Commandments."[6]

Other men of faith did not quite share Adler's belief in the ongoing relevance of the Ten Commandments. Consider the case of Charles Henry Parkhurst, one of New York's leading religious personalities and a longtime crusader against urban vice, who, one Sunday morning in 1908, raised a lot of hackles (and eyebrows too) when he suggested from the pulpit of the prestigious Madison Square Presbyterian Church that perhaps it was high time to dispense with the Ten Commandments. "I suppose the Decalogue was given in order that it might demonstrate its own futility," he glumly told his parishioners, adding that it had not succeeded millennia ago and was "not held in any excess of respect even today." There was no point in hanging on to the ancient biblical covenant. It simply did not work. Parkhurst's sermon unsettled those who occupied the pews of his church that Sunday morning, as well as those who read about it the next day, when the *New York Times* briskly observed that the clergyman "Calls Decalogue Futile," sending shock waves throughout the city and engendering considerable speculation about what might have precipitated these remarks. What could Parkhurst have been thinking? Had the good reverend, whose many fans once likened him to the "Chrysostom of Madison Avenue," thanks to his unstinting efforts on behalf of civic reform, thrown in the towel and given up on his fellow man? Had the author of *The Sunny Side of Christianity* fallen into a "blue funk"? Or could he be toying with everyone, his remarks a publicity stunt of sorts designed to train the spotlight on the Decalogue? For all the supposition, Parkhurst's motivations remained unclear. If his desired intention was to stir the waters, he succeeded. For a few days in May, the Ten Commandments were the talk of the town.[7]

But not for long. With so much else on their minds, most average New Yorkers were not inclined to expend much energy mulling over the Ten Commandments. They left that to the biblical scholar and the biblical archaeologist, whose increasingly sophisticated efforts at interpreting the Old Testament generated steadily growing interest in whether the "thought expressed in the Bible does in fact convey truth." Did the ancient text "correspond with the discoveries of the astronomer, the geologist, and especially the archaeologist?" wondered P. W. Wilson within the pages of the *New York Times*. Some, especially the "perniciously advanced" American disciples of Wellhausen and his school of biblical criticism, answered with a resounding no. They firmly believed that advances in philology, coupled with a recent spate of arresting archaeological discoveries in the Middle East, threw cold water on the historicity of Moses and, most especially, on the timelessness of his proscriptions. The Ten Commandments, they argued, were never meant to serve as a foundational document for all of mankind, let alone for the citizens of the United States of America. The biblical covenant was a product of the ancient Near East—of a particular place and time, as well as a specific set of circumstances. A universal text it was not. Ardent believers in positivism, some American biblical critics even dismissed the idea that Moses, with the twin tablets in tow, had made it down from the mountain in the first place. Two ancient stelae, fashioned out of stone, and containing approximately 172 words, would surely have been much too heavy for the aging Moses to bear, said they.[8]

They had a point—but it was not uniformly accepted. Far from it. In what came to resemble a modern-day jousting match, those students of the ancient Near East who had remained true believers and, in the words of the *Methodist Review*, had "not been carried away by the vagaries of Wellhausen and his school," maintained that the "spade confirm[ed] the Bible," rather than buried it. Recent archaeological discoveries in Egypt, Palestine, Asia Minor, and the Euphrates Valley, they insisted, bore "convincingly upon historic incidents in the Scriptures." One of the faithful, Professor Herbert Grimme of the University of Münster, was even confident that he had found the original Ten Commandments among a clutch of broken tablets in an Egyptian tomb. Even though his was decidedly a minority opinion, others within the field of biblical archaeology thought it only a matter of time before the ground would yield hard and fast proof of the veracity of Moses's experiences atop Mount Sinai. In the meantime, the latest archaeological finds had already thrown a "tremendously comforting light on the Biblical record," or so Bishop Horace M. DuBose of the Southern Methodist Episcopal Church would have it. Wherever one's loyalties lay, there was no doubt that by the early twentieth century, knowledge of the broader context in which the Bible took shape was at an all-time high. "The ancient world is almost as well known as the world of today," observed another man of the cloth, Reverend G. H. Richardson, writing in 1916 in the *Biblical World* about the uses, abuses, and virtues of biblical archaeology. Americans, both within and without the academy, "see as never before the world in which [ancient] Israel lived and moved and had its being." When it came to reconciling fact and faith, newfound knowledge might prompt contemporary Americans to adopt an "attitude of readjustment."[9]

Thomas Carver, a Harvard University professor of economics, was among those doing a bit of readjusting. In lieu of casting the Ten Commandments into the dustbin of history, he proposed to contemporize them. America would be well served were it to substitute "Thou shalt not drink," a much more pressing and timely commandment, for "Thou shalt not take the name of the Lord thy God in vain," an increasingly obsolete one, he suggested in 1909. By then, the use of God's name in daily speech had become commonplace rather than sacrilegious. Instead of conceiving of blasphemy as a religious infraction, it was best to chalk it up to a "dwarfed vocabulary" or a lapse in manners. Drinking, though, was something else again: a real threat to society's stability. How about a new commandment mandating temperance? Another academic, E. A. Ross, a professor of sociology at the University of Wisconsin, went his Harvard colleague one better, arguing that Americans should not substitute one commandment for another so much as "enlarge" the Ten Commandments as a whole. Why not add an "annual supplement" of the latest vices that needed to be contained, he recommended.[10]

Neither Ross's nor Carver's recommendations caught fire. But when, in 1922, George Harvey, the American ambassador to the Court of St. James, proposed that women ought to have a Ten Commandments all their own, he nearly created a diplomatic incident. Some called for his head, insisting that he resign his post; others wanted him to be publicly reprimanded. And still others suggested America's representative would do well to leave the Decalogue alone, maintaining that "it was good enough for our forefathers. It is good enough for us." The ambassador disagreed. Certain that he had both "logic and reason," as well as history, on his side, he insisted that the Ten Commandments were written for and applied exclusively to men. After all, back then women had neither rights nor souls. "Either the commandments should be revised to meet the requirements of modern conditions or a specific decalogue should be constructed exclusively for women," he counseled, supplying newspapers on both sides of the pond with a lot to talk about. In an effort to cool things down, several pundits suggested it was all a joke. Harvey was merely "trying to add to the gayety of nations by offering to them a large and elaborate piece of nonsense," opined the *New York Times*.[11]

Women would have none of it. "I was indignant when I first read his speech," Magistrate Jean Norris told the press, "but later I considered the whole business highly absurd." It was not worth dignifying with a reply. Fannie Hurst, the celebrated writer, took a different tack, taking on George Harvey and the rest of his sex. The ambassador's remarks were typical of men everywhere, she observed, noting that "all men have felt . . . that woman was a spare rib, so far as her place in the world's affairs was concerned, while spiritually she has been about as important as a cabbage." But that situation was bound to change as more and more women sought equal rights, she concluded, linking the Harvey incident to broader contemporary concerns and dismissing the idea that the whole thing, from start to finish, was a laughing matter. "Mr. Harvey expressed in his speech just the condition which women are fighting when they champion emancipation."[12]

The state of women's souls may have been up for grabs, but things were clearer, less equivocal, within the animal kingdom. Ernest Thompson Seton, the popular naturalist, author of *Wild Animals I Have Known*, and founder of the "great Wood Craft or Seton Indian Nation," a precursor to the Boy Scouts of America, turned to nature rather than history or diplomacy to shore up the Ten Commandments. Spending time in the wild, amid the company of wolves, bears, rattlesnakes, and hawks, Seton "subjected the rules of Moses to fresh, up-to-date examination." There he discovered that the laws of the animal kingdom bore an unusually close resemblance to those brought down from Mount Sinai, especially the last six of them. "The Ten Commandments are not arbitrary laws given to man, but are fundamental laws of all highly developed animals," the scientist declared conclusively in "The Natural History of the Ten Commandments," an article that first appeared in the November 1907 issue of the high-toned and much-read *Century* magazine and subsequently as a slender book published by Charles Scribner's Sons. In its pages, Seton detailed how animals "instinctively" understood the importance of parental obedience, honored "property rights," took great pains to avoid murdering their own kind, avoided promiscuity, and practiced monogamy, which, he observed, was the "rule among all the highest and most successful animals." By naturalizing the Decalogue, the scientist rendered its provisions an organic part of the universe rather than an artifact of history. His conclusions came as welcome news to those given to fretting about the future of the ancient code. "The Commandments are safe," the *New York Times* reported with considerable relief, noting that Seton's words made for "good reading" and were "admirably reassuring" to boot.[13]

Although it took a naturalist to quiet the nation's doubting Thomases, or at least those who read the *Times,* the Ten Commandments were never in imminent danger of crumbling. Taken on their own, these discussions about naturalizing, historicizing, and contemporizing the covenant did not amount to much. In the face of criticism here and skepticism there, the Ten Commandments held fast. Still, when these slings and arrows are bundled together, viewed cumulatively and over the long haul, one can see how, bit by bit, they did have an impact: a chipping away of the commandments' moral suasion, a weakening of their hold on the American body politic. By the early years of the twentieth century, the Ten Commandments were no longer quite as high and mighty, as invincible, as they had once been. More and more Americans were prepared to entertain the possibility that the Ten Commandments were not the ultimate arbiter, the one and only source of the law and of America's moral order.

At the same time, few Americans were prepared to dispense with them altogether. How could they? The centrality of the Ten Commandments had been drummed into them since childhood, or at least since they were old enough to have attended Sunday school, where they made their way through instructional catechisms. Belief in the Decalogue was not easily surrendered. How, then, to engage with the biblical prescriptions, to reckon with their contingency while also acknowledging their hold on the American imagination? How to balance their staying power with their malleability?

It took some doing, but modern America eventually came up with the perfect solution: it redefined the Ten Commandments as

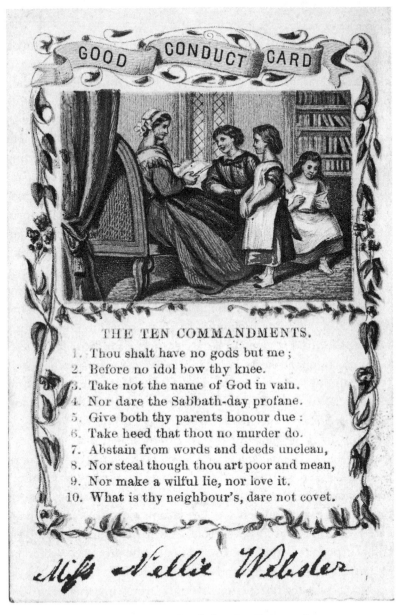

GOOD CONDUCT CARD

THE TEN COMMANDMENTS.

1. Thou shalt have no gods but me ;
2. Before no idol bow thy knee.
3. Take not the name of God in vain.
4. Nor dare the Sabbath-day profane.
5. Give both thy parents honour due :
6. Take heed that thou no murder do.
7. Abstain from words and deeds unclean,
8. Nor steal though thou art poor and mean,
9. Nor make a wilful lie, nor love it.
10. What is thy neighbour's, dare not covet.

Miss Nellie Webster

Whether taught at home or at school, the Ten Commandments were once a central feature of the moral education of American children. Students committed them to memory, declaimed them from the stage, and even put them to song. *Warshaw Collection of Business Americana—Religion, Archives Center, National Museum of American History, Smithsonian Institution* a series of gentle cautions and helpful hints. Brought down from on high and thrust into the center of daily life, where compliance was encouraged rather than mandated, the Ten Commandments were increasingly harnessed to quotidian matters—to piano playing and skin care, driving a car, finding true love, and being a good citizen (or a good anti-Communist). Nothing if not pliable, they lent themselves to new, and decidedly modern, applications. Extending their reach, the Ten Commandments became more boon companion than moral code, a shorthand for the right way of doing things. Less an assertion of divine will than the voice of authority, a form of expertise—and a democratic one at that—they secularized well. "With these Ten Commandments of mine," related Pietro Cimini, a former guest conductor at the Hollywood Bowl in Los Angeles and the author of the 1936 handbook *My Ten Commandments for Correct Voice Production*, "I do not intend to pose as a Moses of the art of music, bringing his pupils to a new revelation, but simply to offer the vocal student a plain, clear set of fundamental rules." Cimini's commandments called for the "erect posture of the body" (commandment number two) and for keeping one's jaw "completely relaxed" (commandment number five). Cimini was in good company. Some twenty years earlier, in 1913, a musical colleague with the arresting name of Platon Brounoff had offered his students *The Ten Commandments of Piano Practice*, an arrangement of ten speedy exercises designed to eliminate "many hours of unnecessary practice." Were a student or his or her piano teacher to keep Brounoff's commandments—the second commandment mandated "diatonic four finger exercises," while the ninth called for a trill of arpeggios—their hands and fingers, he promised, would be in "perfect trim and command of the keyboard."[14]

Music was by no means the only arena in which the Ten Commandments held sway. Unsure of how to grow tomatoes? All you had to do was consult the *Ten Commandments of Pomology*. Affairs of the heart got you down? The soothing harmonies of *The Ten Commandments of Love* could lift your spirits. Determined to fight Communism? *The Ten Commandments of Citizenship* (commandment number ten: "Be Americans First") was a most willing ally. Cultivating interfaith relations high on your civic agenda? The "Ten Commandments of Good-Will," courtesy of the National Conference of Jews and Christians, furnished a helpful template. Urban life much too noisy? Why not arm yourself with *The Ten Commandments of Quiet Automobile Driving,* whose tenets advocated "thinking more and tooting less." Not sure how to maintain a lovely complexion? Helena Rubinstein's compendium of helpful hints, "Ten Commandments to Beauty," was at hand. Adolescent angst standing in the way of happiness? Paul Anka's *The Teen Commandments* just might brighten your day (commandment number nine: "Avoid following the crowd. Be an engine, not a caboose"; commandment number ten: "Keep the original Ten Commandments"). Whatever demons of daily life awaited the average American teenager and his or her parents, the Ten Commandments were at the ready, smoothing the way forward. Even today, imaginative reworkings of the Ten Commandments continue to be thick on the ground, where they are yoked, among other things, to cell phone etiquette ("Thou shalt not use cell phones, text message or play electronic games during [worship] Services") and to proper nutrition ("Thou shall consume protein; thou shalt not consume too much chocolate").[15]

Applying an age-old religious text such as the Bible to contemporary phenomena was, of course, nothing new. You could easily fill a bookshelf or two with the likes of *The Bible of Life Insurance* and *The Bible of the Blues,* whose titles offered the promise of comprehensiveness, much less the patina of authority. But the Ten Commandments offered even more, their structure, language, and sensibility particularly suited to the modern age. Pithy and direct, aphoristic and handy-dandy, the text was of a piece with the snappy advertising copy of the marketplace and the memorable, stay-in-your-head jingles increasingly heard on the radio. In twentieth-century America, everyone at some point or another had heard of

the Ten Commandments; they possessed the *ne plus ultra* in rec-
ognizability. That their authority also derived from numbers furthered their appeal. There was something unassailable, something
unmistakably modern, about a system whose foundation rested
on counting from one to ten. Their neat and tidy formulaity rang
true, appearing to leave little margin for error. At the same time,
any resemblance between the original and its offspring represented
more of a symbolic convergence than a literal one. At no point did
any of the modern-day applications of the Ten Commandments
directly correspond to the original lineup: the second, sixth, and
tenth commandments of good citizenship or skin care did not in
any way align with the second, sixth, and ten commandments of
the version Moses brought down from Mount Sinai, either the first
or the second time around. What inspired latter-day Americans to
make use of the Ten Commandments for their own, earthly ends
was the prospect of clarity and the promise of order that a numerical composition like this one afforded. Taking the sting out of
modern life, the Ten Commandments imposed a structure on its
unpredictability and messiness.

Authority, clarity, and order—the perquisites of stability and
of personal fulfillment. Is it any wonder that in our own day the
Ten Commandments have become a vehicle of self-help, a therapeutic document rather than an expression of transcendence? To
leap from Mount Sinai to the analyst's couch does not seem to
have been too much of a stretch, not if we take the word of radio
commentator Laura Schlessinger and educator David Hazony.
As Schlessinger's 1998 bestseller, *The Ten Commandments: The
Significance of God's Laws in Everyday Life*, which she wrote with
Rabbi Stewart Vogel, and Hazony's well-received 2010 book, *The
Ten Commandments: How Our Most Ancient Moral Text Can Renew
Modern Life*, attest, the biblical sayings might well be the perfect
antidote for what ails us. "The Ten Commandments seem like an
excellent formula for making one a 'better person,'" Schlessinger
declared, adding that they serve as a "moral focal point for

thousands of real-life issues, including relating to God, family, our fellows, sex, work, charity, property, speech, and thought." Chatty and affable in tone, she drew on a range of sources, from biblical texts to the on-air comments and letters composed by Americans named Becky, Cindy, Murray, and Paul, to show how and why the Ten Commandments remained relevant to modern-day America—and good for us too. Each commandment offered a contemporary life lesson, an opportunity to take stock and do better. Punctuated by familiar catchphrases on the order of "Have you hugged your kids lately?," "Adultery: just say no," and "Time-out!," Schlessinger's account popularized the Ten Commandments, setting them squarely within the grooves of daily life where Becky, Cindy, Murray, and Paul were encouraged to dust them off and use them as a "blueprint of God's expectations upon us and His plan for a meaningful, just, loving and holy life."[16]

Hazony too insisted on their relevance. Far more elegant and learned than Schlessinger, he was just as determined as she to turn the Ten Commandments from an "abstract vision into something concrete and pragmatic." Chapter by chapter, commandment by commandment, the Jerusalem-based critic suggested how each one might figure as a "biblical affirmation of the self" (aka the fourth commandment) and as a "revelation about ourselves" (aka the first commandment). Notionally about the Decalogue, Hazony's account placed the individual at the center of his narrative, inviting him or her to view the Ten Commandments as a template of personal uplift, a measure of confidence building. "Every commandment," he exuberantly affirmed, "represents a whole world of value, an awakening of the redemptive spirit in its own arena of life."[17]

As the Ten Commandments steadily came into their own as "redemptive spirits" and autonomous agents, so too did the tangible, visual forms in which they appeared. No longer the sole preserve of the church, the synagogue, and the Sunday school, where they were statically and somberly featured in a sanctuary and a classroom, representations of the Ten Commandments grew more commonplace and livelier too: more colloquial, less august. Shorn of their exclusively religious connotations, they blossomed into appurtenances of the everyday: bookmarks, book covers, comic books, good conduct cards, postcards, and lavishly illustrated chromolithographs hung just so in a parlor or a bedroom. Today, many of these items can be found in archives and museums where their artful blend of form and function, of tradition and modernity, catches the eye.

Mine fastened on a late nineteenth-century bookmark fashioned out of celluloid, or what we know today as plastic. On a narrow strip of the most-up-to-date material of its time, the age-old biblical text looms large; it takes up much of the surface space. A quasi-ecclesiastical object perhaps? One used by a member of the clergy in the course of a homily, or its preparation, so that he might easily find his place when citing chapter and verse? A closer and more sustained look at this artifact gives rise to a different interpretation, one that might just as effectively situate it within a sitting room, whose occupants dreamily read a novel, than in a house of worship, where those in the pews strained to hear. At the top or crown of this bookmark sits a flower—a rose—in full bloom, looking as if it is ready to be plucked. It beckons, lush and inviting and a tad mysterious too, for it is not at all clear how these floralized Ten Commandments were meant to be read. Those readers familiar with the language of flowers and its Christological associations might be inclined to see this particular rose as an expression of faith, as an example of what Leigh Schmidt, a historian of American religious culture, calls "floral piety," a visual practice and language that spoke of rebirth and redemption.[18]

They would be right to think so. This bookmark, after all, was of a piece with the steady incorporation of flowers into the late nineteenth- and early twentieth-century celebration of Christian holidays, when they adorned holiday greeting cards, advertisements, home décor, and, most especially, church interiors at Easter. "The festival, coming as it does in early spring, is best

Pretty to look at and practical too, this bookmark married the ancient wisdom of the Bible to the technological innovation of celluloid, an early form of plastic. *Division of Medicine & Science, National Museum of American History, Smithsonian Institution, 2006.0098.0655*

Brightly colored, cheery chromolithographs of the Ten Commandments became increasingly popular in late nineteenth- and early twentieth-century America, adding to the repertoire of affordable parlor art. *Warshaw Collection of Business Americana—Religion, Archives Center, National Museum of American History, Smithsonian Institution*

commemorated by the use of as many flowers as possible," recommended Ernest R. Suffling, whose 1907 manual, *Church Festival Decorations: Being Full Directions for Garnishing Churches for Christmas, Easter, Whitsuntide and Harvest,* offered a plethora of seasonal suggestions. The anonymous creator of the floralized Ten Commandments bookmark appears to have taken Suffling's directions to heart, beautifying the ancient legal code even while situating it within a domestic context. Contemporary readers would also be right in thinking there is room here for another, more free-floating reading, one that endows the flower with personal rather than religious meaning. The floral image of a rose atop the Ten Commandments hints at growth rather than stasis, at possibility rather than punishment. It domesticates the Ten Commandments, placing them well within reach.[19]

I was drawn to another floralized version of the Decalogue—a poster destined to be hung on a wall rather than a piece of plastic tucked inside a book. It too was a state-of-the-art affair, a testament to the visual power of chromolithography. Awash in color, in saturated pinks and vibrant greens, it planted the Ten Commandments in a garden of flowers and branches. To gild the lily, cameos of ordinary people, some in ancient garb, others in modern dress, accompanied each commandment to illustrate its meaning. There is a lot to take in. But, then, that is the point. This busy composition, rich in human incident and vibrant detail, was at once an opportunity for storytelling and an exercise in visual expression. Like the floral bookmark, this image brought the Ten Commandments down to earth, where they are softened, even feminized. The impact of its portrayal is felt more keenly when you consider what is missing: a rock-ribbed Mount Sinai or a hardened Moses is nowhere to be seen. Even the presence of the stone tablets was muted; at one with their surroundings, they blended in rather than stood out. By stripping the Ten Commandments of their harsh, stony, patriarchal qualities and replacing them with a string of warm and familial associations, this particular chromolithograph suggested that the

Ten Commandments had more to do with affirmation than with accountability. They were full of promise.[20]

The taming of the Ten Commandments similarly affected the ways in which Americans related to Moses, their standard bearer. Likened over time to a Greek god, but better; to the nation's favorite foundling; to a voodoo priest; to a "kind of American Hamlet"; and to "one of the greatest salesmen . . . that ever lived," as the Metropolitan Casualty Life Insurance's pamphlet, *Moses: Persuader of Men*, blithely would have it, the biblical figure was increasingly transformed from a distant figure on a mountaintop into an accessible and all-too-human character of great and abiding appeal to children, who, more often than not, encountered him within the pages of a comic book or held him in their hands. Where the traditional view of Moses presented him as seasoned and stern, with discipline his stock-in-trade, the Moses befriended by American children of the twentieth century was plucky and resolute; adventure was his calling card.[21]

Take *Moses and the Ten Commandments*, a Dell Comics publication, for example. Drawing on the gee-whiz, exclamation-ridden cadences of the genre, as well as its customary visual properties, it not only set Moses within the company of other superheroes but also translated his story into a modern coming-of-age drama. The plot, which took its cue and contours from the biblical story, with a gentle nod in the direction of Cecil B. DeMille's 1956 film, had largely to do with Moses's varied adventures. These anchored and shaped the narrative as it moved at a fast clip from the stages of boyhood and adolescence into that of "confident manhood." A boyish Moses cannot keep his shirt (or tunic) in his pants; he drinks lots of milk; he asks too many questions, especially those having to do with Mother Nature; and he gets into—and out of—numerous scrapes with various and sundry authority figures. Quick-witted, he is equally quick with his fists and knows how to land a finely placed punch. Most tellingly, Moses is quite comely. Shown to advantage in a loincloth, of all things, his body is finely chiseled and muscular;

his eyes are blue and piercing and his hair full and inky blank. Even when his brow begins to furrow and he takes to wearing yards of striped fabric—a mark not only of his getting on in years but also of his increasing seriousness—his body retains its youthful build. In the course of things, Moses stares down a mighty lion, rights society's wrongs, acquires a new identity as an Israelite, squares off against a nasty pharaoh, sees his people to safety, and, as an added bonus, receives the Ten Commandments. It is hard to keep up with him. By all accounts, he leads a full and action-packed existence: a "WOW" of a life.[22]

Ultimately, though, what registers most profoundly within the pages of this densely packed comic page is not the fullness of Moses's career, but process—the process of becoming. Within the world of the comic book, little is static. Moses, and we its readers, along with him, are in a continuous state of movement: from boy to man, from Egyptian to Israelite, from prince to a representative of God Almighty. In each instance, Moses's life is defined as an exercise in maturation: in how to become a grown-up and assume responsibility.

Moses the action figure picks up where the comic book leaves off. It too makes much of adventure. "The story of Moses has more action than a James Bond movie," trills one website that features the doll. "Miracles, murder, plagues, escape, betrayal—his life was filled with dramatic events and exciting adventures." Another website, sounding just like a comic book, down to its excessive use of exclamation points, gushes: "He hooked us up with the Ten Commandments. He delivered the Jews from slavery! He parted the Red Sea! He lived to be 120! What can't he do? You too can feel the power!" This paragon of possibility stands a "commanding" five and one-quarter inches tall and can "articulate" his joints in at least sixteen different directions. His flexible musculature, we are told, empowers him to "hang with your Spiderman, Batman and Superman." Though he is in good company, Moses differs from his compatriots in the manner of his dress. Where they consistently sport capes and tights, Moses action figures vary their attire and "accoutrements," as the toy industry rather grandly puts it. Some prototypes feature a world-weary, heavily bearded Moses clad in a flowing robe and sturdy sandals. At other moments, he resembles a souped-up Roman gladiator. Often, Moses stands alone and unencumbered; he can also be found wielding a staff, a set of the Ten Commandments, and other "authentic archaeological objects." On occasion, he even lugs around a portable burning bush or comes equipped with "Biblically based biographical info" conferring on him a *soupçon* of authenticity.[23]

Whatever its pedigree, the Moses action figure was intended as a peaceable alternative to the gun-toting, kick-in-the-groin antics of his counterparts. It was also intended to insinuate religion into the rhythms of daily life by "providing Bible storytelling possibilities" alongside moments of "playtime fun." With the Moses action figure, prospective consumers were told, "you can recreate the entire epic saga in the comfort of your own home." Besides, if you happened to be Jewish, there was no better way to maximize the appeal of and enhance the Passover Seder than by adding a Moses action figure to the guest list. "This pint sized hero can bring a miraculous new level of excitement to your Seder," advertisements boasted with a straight face, holding out the possibility that fun and games with Moses might banish the inevitable ritual ennui. I don't know about that. It seems a lot to ask of a doll. What I do know, though, is that Moses action figures humanized the ancient biblical hero, placing him squarely within the warp and woof of the everyday, where he came into his own as a buddy, someone fun to have around the house.[24]

From cutting Moses down to size and floralizing the Ten Commandments to rendering them an instrument of daily life, their history in modern America might well be seen as a woeful tale of diminution, perhaps even of desacralization and corruption. To conjure up an image of Moses high-fiving his compatriots or dispensing advice about skin care is, arguably, not a pretty picture.

Long before the heroic Moses became an action figure, Americans drew on images of the baby Moses to tout the soothing properties of both motherhood and of nostrums designed to relieve a wide variety of ailments. *Library of Congress, Prints and Photographs Division, LC-DIG-ppmsca-09485*

Surely, you think to yourself, this was not what he—or the good Lord—intended when the Ten Commandments first saw the light of day. Paradoxically enough, however, the vernacular embrace of the divine commandments represented an expansion rather than a delimiting of their circumference. By the mid-twentieth century, no area of modern life was without a Ten Commandments of its own. Lodged within every nook and cranny of American life, rendered into language that everyone understood, and applied to ordinary circumstances rather than heroic measures, the Ten Commandments had metamorphosed into America's ultimate to-do list.

Chapter Three

Good Neighbors

May 18, 1850, was a banner day in the life of Congregation Anshi Chesed, a traditional synagogue in the heart of New York's *kleine Deutschland*, the city's preeminent German neighborhood. Several hundred of the congregation's members, along with some of the city's most prominent officials and a "great many other persons of distinction," gathered together on that spring afternoon, crowding the area's narrow byways, to dedicate the congregation's spanking new building on Norfolk Street. Clutching a small card of admission—"not transferable," it read—they jostled for admission to the Gothic Revival–style synagogue, the largest in the city, a structure whose ambitious proportions dwarfed all the other buildings in its immediate vicinity. A proud, and decidedly modern, urban presence, Anshi Chesed, also known as the Norfolk Street Synagogue, was said to be in step with the "progressive feelings of the age," as well as the very last word in stylishness. Its architect, Alexander Saeltzer, had made sure of it. An up-and-coming professional in his early thirties who hailed from and was trained in Berlin and who, only a few short years later, would go on to erect New York's storied Astor Library and its Academy of Music, Saeltzer adorned the exterior of his red-brick building with "ornamented turrets" and its interior with a "mammoth," three-tiered chandelier from which hung forty-eight gas jets, then the height of novelty.[1]

The Norfolk Street Synagogue also contained a prominently situated stained-glass window that depicted the Ten Commandments.

As stunning as the building's exterior turrets and as modern as its chandelier, it floated right above the ark that contained the Torah scrolls, commanding the attention of those seated in the pews below. The window's unusual shape also drew the eye. Instead of embedding the ten prescriptions within the rigid and customary geometry of two tablets, Saeltzer had them marching freely within the circumference of a circle. These Ten Commandments were in the round. More like the spokes of a wheel than the flat inscriptions on a stele, each "Thou shalt" and "Thou shalt not" was housed within its own unit of glass. To heighten the effect, a series of ten petal-shaped panels occupied the center of the composition.

A rose window by any other name, the synagogue's stained-glass salute to the Decalogue cascaded bands of color unto the ark, illumining it much as the Ten Commandments illumined Jewish life. You could almost hear the architect talking up the fine points of his creation: how its circularity expanded the space; brought abundant light into the sanctuary; represented a modern, more inclusive use of one of the cardinal principles of ecclesiastical design; and signaled the congregation's forward-looking approach to modern Jewish life, its willingness to open itself up to new ideas and abstractions even as it remained true to its faith. The press agreed, singling out the window for high praise in its account of the dedication ceremonies. "This stained glass has a very pleasing effect," observed the *New-York Daily Tribune*, whose detailed coverage of the proceedings ran to six columns of newsprint. "The Commandments, instead of being on two tablets, are each on a separate pane of glass, around the window, surmounting the Ark," it pointed out. The *Asmonean*, a weekly New York Jewish newspaper nearly as new as the Norfolk Street building, felt the same way. It too highlighted the unusual configuration of the window, noting how it "diffused a pleasant hue over the gay array of blooming faces with which the galleries were crowded."[2]

Thrilled at first by the positive publicity, the members of Anshi Chesed soon changed their tune and, in the time-honored tradition

The grand proportions and handsome design of the antebellum Norfolk Street synagogue in New York made its congregants feel welcome and at home in the United States. *Archives of the Angel Orensanz Foundation*

of congregants everywhere, began to grumble and murmur darkly about their distinctively configured Ten Commandments window. The minutes of the synagogue, which dutifully record this and other instances of congregational dissension, contain scarcely a clue about the identity of the naysayers. Did they represent the more pious members of the congregation? The more recently arrived? The minutes are also frustratingly silent on what set things off. Surely, Anshi Chesed's congregants, or at least those who served on the building committee or on its board of trustees, knew in advance of their sanctuary's consecration what the Ten Commandments window was going to look like. It was unlikely that the first time they set eyes on or heard about it was at its public unveiling, especially since Saeltzer had consistently made a point of showing the synagogue board a series of drawings of the sanctuary's other features. Then again, as anyone who has ever worked with an architect or an interior designer knows all too well, there is often a gap—a big one—between what the client has in mind (or understands) and what the artist actually devises. Perhaps this is what happened between the congregants at Anshi Chesed and their architect, and that growing discontent with his depiction of the Ten Commandments was rooted in a difference of both perception and expectation.

Establishing what they knew and when they knew it is an elusive bit of business. But one thing is certain. Once they beheld their newly consecrated Ten Commandments window, a vocal contingent of worshippers insisted it had to go, hang the expense and the architect's feelings. Did they find it ugly? Ungainly? Much too showy and colorful? Perhaps even a tad irreverent? Were they concerned that Saeltzer's rendition did the Ten Commandments a disservice, rendering them too abstract, too novel, too modern by half? Would they have preferred to have dispatched them in marble rather than in stained glass, and in the shape of a rectangular tablet rather than a circle? Would they have wanted to see them affixed to the ark, their usual placement, rather than hover above it? Questions beget more questions—but few answers. Once again, the extant sources give us no information. Clearly, though, something about the Ten Commandments window did not pass muster with the Jews of Norfolk Street.

As momentum for its displacement accelerated, Anshi Chesed's lay leaders decided to quell further dissent within their ranks by forming a committee. The committee approach to problem solving had recently become a regular feature of the congregation or *shul*, as it styled itself in Hebrew in its minute books. Committees sprang up like mushrooms, a testament to its newfound democratic ethos: there was a committee to monitor decorum, especially among the "ladies" who were "requested earnestly to abstain entirely from holding loud conversations during divine service," and a committee to look into the prospect of introducing gaslight into the Norfolk Street building as a whole, a committee to purchase a clock and one to distribute spittoons. And now, dutifully drawing on the Hebrew words for the Ten Commandments, Anshi

Chesed decided to constitute its very own "Committee on *Aseres hadebros*," whose members—Messrs. Abrahams, Bernheimer, and Stern, but not a Moses among the three of them—set out to repair the situation. Contemporary readers might find the name of the committee somewhat presumptuous and its mandate a particularly amusing proposition, but at the time nobody looked askance. Those who appointed the committee, and those who constituted it, took their charge quite seriously.[3]

As its first order of business, the Committee on *Aseres hadebros* sought the counsel of "competent persons" to determine what the Ten Commandments should actually look like. By "competent persons," the committee did not have in mind an artist or even a biblical scholar so much as a rabbi—which, at the time, they lacked. The previous incumbent, Max Lilienthal, had resigned his post in a huff shortly before the congregation had decided to build itself a sparkling new facility, and he had not been replaced. Bereft of a rabbinic presence, Anshi Chesed managed to fend for itself in most things, trusting to its lay leaders. But this unwieldy situation called for an authoritative voice, someone with the clout and standing to resolve it, once and for all. Accordingly, the Committee on *Aseres hadebros* sought the counsel of a higher religious authority (whose name, curiously enough, was not recorded), to whom they put the following question: "Whether the Ten Commandments (*Aseres hadebros*), as they are fixed at present, may remain as they are, painted in a circle on stained glass or if it is against the *din* (Jewish law) and ought to be fixed in the usual way on two tablets?" By framing their question as a matter of Jewish law, they looked for a rabbinic seal of approval on their distinctively shaped Decalogue: was it kosher or not?[4]

Much to its disappointment, the answer the committee received—and in relatively quick order, suggesting that its author lived in America—did little to resolve the congregation's quandary. The rabbinic response read, somewhat lumberingly: "There was nothing in the laws which prescribes any form, consequently, that it is not against the *din* to have them fixed as they are at present, but that they are, as a general thing, fixed differently, namely on two tablets, and that they have never been seen put up in a circle." Anshi Chesed's members wanted to know categorically whether there was a right way or a wrong way to depict the Ten Commandments. But in lieu of a flat-out, clear-cut ruling, they were told yes *and* no. Yes, the version of the Decalogue that adorned the interior of the Norfolk Street synagogue was highly unusual, but no, it did not contravene Jewish law. This was not at all what they wanted to hear. They had hoped for a definitive statement; they received a nuanced one instead.[5]

And there the matter rested. But not for long. In the months that followed, many of the worshippers who occupied the pews of the Norfolk Street synagogue continued to feel uneasy in the presence of their newfangled Ten Commandments. Adding to their discomfort, they had gotten wind of some really bad press written by a gentleman who styled himself "Honestus." A visit to Anshi Chesed had left him in such a state of high dudgeon that he felt compelled to put pen to paper and rail: "I have observed of late, a disposition on the part of certain Israelites . . . to attempt what they term *improvements* in matters and things appertaining to our religion." But they go too far and end up "obliterat[ing]" those "peculiar characteristics that has [*sic*] ever marked, and in my opinion ought to mark, the Jewish place of worship," he wrote hotly within the pages of the high-toned *Occident and American Jewish Advocate*, invoking Congregation Anshi Chesed, whose much-vaunted stained-glass window represented a glaring, and woeful, instance of this contemporary trend. As Honestus would have it: "So great has been the desire for originality and improvement, that the very Ten Commandments, which have always been written on tablets to resemble the shape we are accustomed to see . . . are altogether divested of their outward character that could the prophet himself see them, I question his being able to recognize them in their new and novel appearance." Anathematizing novelty, Honestus's blistering attack made it seem as if Congregation Anshi Chesed had committed the most egregious of sins: deliberately cutting itself off from its roots, even turning its back on Moses.[6]

Amid such fierce and fighting words, some of the more unsettled members of the community picked up the gauntlet Honestus threw down and, determined to reestablish their synagogue's bona fides, its fidelity to tradition, began to agitate anew for the window's removal. Its champions, meanwhile, stood their ground. They liked what they saw and were not about to relinquish this decidedly modern version of the ancient text without a fight, Honestus and his opinion be damned. Besides, the cost of removing the window would have been prohibitive. The congregation was already in debt and in the protracted process of paying the bills of its architect and bricklayer, plasterer and upholsterer, and, and, and. It simply could not afford the expense of taking down this stained-glass Decalogue and replacing it with another.

Lest matters continue to fester, splintering the congregation in two, the synagogue's lay leaders came up with a plan that was nothing short of Solomonic. To satisfy its champions (and architect), the window would be retained. But to satisfy its detractors, the Committee on *Aseres hadebros* was reinstated and charged with a new mandate: To "get tablets made and to have the *Aseres hadebros* inscribed therein as it is more appropriate to have them fixed so"— which it did. In an eerie evocation of the biblical story in which Moses, having angrily dashed the first set of tablets on the ground, ends up fashioning another set, the Norfolk Street Synagogue followed suit, augmenting its original commission with a second one. Like their ancestors of yore, these latter-day Israelites of the Lower East Side could also claim a multiple set of Decalogues to their name. With history on their side, they now boasted two in-house versions of the Ten Commandments: an innovatively styled, circular Ten Commandments rendered out of stained glass and a traditional set of tablets, fashioned out of marble, which, as the minutes somewhat inelegantly put it, were "finished in the style as agreed upon [by the] committee on this business." Set squarely atop the ark, the more customary position, the new tablets acted as a counterbalance to the autonomous, eye-catching stained-glass window. Its impact dulled, the visual equivalent of a second fiddle, the latter remained, untouched and intact, well into the 1970s when vandals made off with it, leaving a series of gaping holes where once the Ten Commandments had diffused a pleasant hue.[7]

At first blush, what happened at Anshi Chesed in 1850 is a familiar enough story: a modern gesture, be it aesthetic or liturgical, comes aground on the shoals of tradition. On Norfolk Street, tradition—or what the minutes characterized as the "usual," or the more "appropriate," way—took its cue, as well as its form, from the Bible, where the Ten Commandments were tersely described as being inscribed on two stone tablets, no more, no less. Anything else, any alternative interpretation of either materiel or form, would seem to fall wide of the mark, outside the pale of Judaism, both literally and symbolically. The congregation's novel Ten Commandments, neither fashioned out of stone nor resembling a tablet, contravened tradition at every turn. No wonder its members had misgivings; they had history, much less Moses, to answer to.

But there is more to the story than resistance to change or the heavy hand of the past. What distinguishes this particular breach of tradition from any other is its physicality or, more to the point, its relationship to shape. A circular Ten Commandments, unlike anything the congregants of Norfolk Street or, for that matter, other American Jews had ever encountered before—and have not encountered since—shook things up. A statement of contemporaneity rather than historicity, it startled rather than reassured. The novelty of its shape heralded change rather than constancy, threatening to undo the comforting, and familiar, symmetry of the age-old text. The Ten Commandments, after all, were meant to last. A symbol of permanence and continuity—an avatar of stability—as well as a covenant, the tablets were intended to endure through

the ages. Time yielded to the Ten Commandments, not the other
way around.

A circular Ten Commandments upset the established, time-
worn order of things. It was also hard to read. Given its circularity, you could not easily tell where one commandment began and
another left off: In which direction—right or left—did they move?
Clockwise? Counterclockwise? As much a symbolic challenge as
a literal one, Saeltzer's vision occluded the parallelism with which
the Jews had long understood the relationship between the first
and second halves of the ten prescriptions. At Norfolk Street, parallelism went out the window: goodbye to all that. To compound
matters, the compact size of each pane of glass did not allow much
room for a full transcription of the text, making it hard, now, as
then, to discern which commandment was which. Were they num-
bered one through ten, or I through X, or, better yet, *aleph* through
yud? Did they draw on the first word or two of each commandment? Contemporary sources do not tell us; they are mute on the
matter. Studying what remains of the window is not much help
either. Only its silhouette, shrouded in plastic, remains on view
these days at the Angel Orensanz Foundation, which now inhabits
the building.

I was determined to see for myself, an adventure that had me
first dangling precariously from a topmost balcony in an effort to
get as close to the window as possible and then high up on an exterior rickety fire escape trying to see from the back of the window
what I could not make out from the front. Like those before me,
I had difficulty in figuring out the literal expression of Saeltzer's
scheme. I strained to match various images in my mind's eye to the
space and came up empty-handed. I descended from my perilous
perch, none the wiser and no closer to resolving this artistic puzzle.

My exertions did yield something, though. Apart from relief on
being on solid ground, I took away with me a heightened understanding of the window's symbolic import and with it, a greater

understanding of where it fell short. By emphasizing the circularity of the Ten Commandments, the architect had sought to enhance the fluidity, the resonance, of the millennial words. Round and round they went, from one generation to the next: always relevant, always in play. A noble conceit, to be sure, but something got lost in translation, a sacrifice to visual innovation: legibility.[8]

Instead of inspiring the congregants of Norfolk Street, the unprecedented circularity of these Ten Commandments mystified them. It disrupted the meaning of the ancient prescriptions so completely that these antebellum American Jews did not know what they were looking at: were these Ten Commandments intended as a theological assertion or as a design element? Making much of their confusion, the Norfolk Street congregants extrapolated further, hitching the fate of their stained-glass window to the future of American Judaism. They came to see their Decalogue, its roundness in full flower, as a slippery slope. If the shape of the Ten Commandments could be altered beyond recognition, they wondered fretfully, what of the future of Judaism? Might it shift its shape too? That prospect, a leap of faith, was one that Congregation Anshi Chesed was not quite willing to contemplate, much less make.

And that was just the half of it. As it turned out, the "usual way" of rendering the Ten Commandments encompassed both American and Jewish traditions. Drawing on scriptural precedents, most New Yorkers conceived of the Ten Commandments as a set of tablets. The stuff of altarpieces, illustrated prayer books, Sunday school primers, clocks, watch fobs, and needlepoint samplers, as well as churchly stained-glass windows, the Decalogue was envisioned, time and again, in rectangular terms. By the mid-nineteenth century, its geometrical proportions were fixed, not fluid, prompting the nation's Christians to identify the Ten Commandments with two tablets. As far as the disgruntled members of Congregation Anshi Chesed were concerned, it was worrisome enough that their circular window did not conform to traditional Jewish depictions of the Ten Commandments. That it did not conform to American notions of the Ten Commandments either generated a double whammy of a predicament. The oddly shaped Ten Commandments enhanced rather than subdued the mysteriousness of the Jews.[9]

That state of affairs, or "business," as the minutes briskly put it, could not be countenanced, especially in New York in the 1850s, where the prospect of finding common ground was increasingly touted as a social good, a benefit to both Jews and Christians. "It is pleasant to observe," observed the *Christian Examiner* only a few short months before Anshi Chesed's consecration, that the "Israelites appear to be fast wearing away their most cherished peculiarities." Though Christians had, "for ages," seen the Jews as "morose, narrow, unsocial and exclusive . . . stand[ing] aloof from what interests other people," that characterization was fast losing steam as comity replaced friction and toleration supplanted suspicion. The "free exchange of social relations" was one way to accomplish that. Another was to attend each other's services from time to time. A third was to celebrate and highlight the Ten Commandments, one of the few religious symbols Jews and Christians had in common. Its ten mutually agreed-upon prescriptions made for good neighbors.[10]

Although Christianity had long made a point of superseding the practices and values that characterized the religion from which it had first emerged, it retained the Ten Commandments, heralding them as the direct and unmediated words of God. It kept them close. In the New World, under the sway of Protestantism and its reverence for the Old Testament, it kept them closer still, so much so that this covenant with the ancient Hebrews and their descendants, which resided at the core of their way of life, was now reconfigured as a covenant with America. Once particularistic, the Ten Commandments had become nationalized.

America's Jews did not seem to mind in the least. On the contrary: they delighted in the prominence that America bestowed on the Ten Commandments, relishing the ways in which the national narrative now accommodated the special circumstances of Jewish history. Here, after all, was something the Jews had given the nation: the ultimate gift—a foundational document.

When seen from this angle, Anshi Chesed's anxiety over the appropriateness of its Ten Commandments window made perfect sense. An exercise in self-consciousness, of looking over its shoulder, of peering outside, the congregation's worried response to its innovatively shaped Decalogue was not borne of interfaith dialogue or outreach; that would come later, much later. Rather, it was an expression of concern about what the neighbors would think. Although the congregation's deliberations took place within its immediate precincts, its intended audience was as much the greater public, the readers, say, of the *New-York Daily Tribune*, as it was those who sat in the pews of the sanctuary, served on committees, or read *The Asmonean*, a paper that portrayed the Jews as "friends of true liberty, the lovers of everything that is good." At stake was the twinned dilemma of the American Jew: How best to present Judaism as a modern faith, whose tenets it shared with other inhabitants of the public square? And how, at the same time, to remain honest and true to the claims of a singular tradition? The Jews of Norfolk Street were caught in the middle. Gingerly making their way between two iterations of the Ten Commandments, one whose more traditional form highlighted its consonance with America, and another whose unusual configuration reinforced their "peculiarities," they faced a Hobson's choice: embracing a shared idiom or courting distinctiveness, fitting right in or standing apart.[11]

In the end, Congregation Anshi Chesed's congregants were not quite ready to endorse one opportunity at the expense of the other. Instead, they sought to accommodate them both, hence the two versions of the Ten Commandments. But this balancing act, this attempt at equilibrium, did not take place without a struggle. What happened on Norfolk Street in the years before the Civil

War not only underscored the power of shape to stir things up but also dramatized the tensions inherent in becoming a modern American Jew, tangibly rendering them through the translucence of glass, the weightiness of stone, and the forceful presence of the Ten Commandments.

Fifty-four years later. Another synagogue dedication. Another Ten Commandments fashioned out of stained glass. Another opportunity to lay claim to America. But this time, things were different. This Ten Commandments window graced the fifteen-hundred-seat sanctuary of Congregation Sherith Israel, an avowedly progressive congregation in downtown San Francisco, whose technologically advanced interior was defined by a thousand light bulbs rather than by forty-eight gas jets. For another thing, the debut of this Ten Commandments window in 1905 was greeted with acclamation rather than controversy. A source of pride, not discomfort, it was heartily welcomed by the community; it even bore the seal of rabbinic approval. Some, in fact, have actually credited the congregation's rabbi, Jacob Nieto, with its design. And for a third, this version of the Ten Commandments was no puzzling abstraction, whose meaning was up for grabs. This window, visible to passersby on the street, told a story, pure and simple: how Moses, with the twin tablets in tow, set foot on American soil—or, more precisely still, how the ancient lawgiver came to be in California.

There, in that part of the country commonly referred to as a "second Canaan," the members of Congregation Sherith Israel, many of whom had arrived in the West on the heels of the gold rush, just about the time the congregants of Anshi Chesed were settling into their seats, commissioned a stained-glass window that unequivocally expressed their belief in the United States as the Promised Land and in the Ten Commandments as an American institution. Unambiguous in its claims, Congregation Sherith Israel's half-moon-shaped stained-glass window was the handiwork of Emile Pissis, a local artist who had trained in Paris, owned a studio that was the envy of his fellow painters, and liked to depict scenes of California history. His other claim to fame was familial rather than artistic: Emile's brother, Albert, was among San Francisco's most acclaimed architects, or "blue print men." It was he who designed the capacious California Street synagogue, whose bulbous dome "could be seen from all over the city," or so boasted Rabbi Nieto in an interview with the *London Jewish Chronicle*. Working together (apparently, a rare occurrence), the brothers Pissis constructed and decorated a building that saluted the collective success of West Coast Jewry.[12]

Like so many others before it, Pissis's depiction featured Moses, his long hair and flowing red robe blowing in the wind, his right hand clutching the two tablets to his heart, as he descends from

Setting Moses against the background of Yosemite and American flags, this luminous piece of stained glass—the handiwork of a California artist—reaffirmed American Jewry's unabashed belief in the United States as the Promised Land. *Congregation Sherith Israel, San Francisco; Richard Mayer, photographer*

Mount Sinai. With the exception of a ribbon of electric bulbs that encircled the top of the window, his account seemed to resemble every other Moses-descending-from-Sinai image that had, for decades, bedecked stained-glass windows, chromolithographs, playing cards, and children's illustrated books, even down to the familiar detail of Moses's strappy sandals. But look again. For one thing, the banners held aloft by the tribes who greet the lawgiver at the foot of the mountain were colored red, white, and blue. For another, the flora and fauna that lay underfoot were indigenous to California, not the Middle East. More strikingly still, it was not Mount Sinai that took center stage in the composition, as one might expect, but El Capitan, the craggy, three-thousand-foot rock formation at Yosemite National Park, that "mountain cathedral" hailed by one awestruck tourist as "God's own handiwork."[13]

Crowding the picture plane, El Capitan displaced Mount Sinai, and yet no one blinked an eye, wrung their hands, or uttered a word in protest at this restaging—or was it an upstaging?—of the biblical story. No Honestus appeared on the scene to challenge its legitimacy. One could, of course, argue that Pissis's exuberantly, unabashedly Americanized rendition was of a piece with the centuries-old pictorial tradition of using local topographical and sartorial conventions to depict ancient practices, peoples, and places. Illuminated manuscripts of the Haggadah or those of *Megillat Esther*, the Scroll of Esther, are replete with instances in which the Jews of antiquity were envisioned as if they were the latter-day Jews of Sarajevo or Cologne who had commissioned them in the first place: at once an expression of continuity, of timelessness, as well as a testament to the limits of the imagination. In the medieval and early modern era, people drew what they knew.

Pissis's decidedly modern representation, on the other hand, was something else entirely: an expansion of the imagination rather than its contraction. By the time he created a model, selected his palette, and found the right kind of opalescent glass to contain his vision, much was known about the ancient Near East. Travel accounts, Bibles festooned with representative samples of flora and fauna, photographs and stereopticon slides of the Holy Land, as well as stone specimens, courtesy of the American Holy-Land Exploration Society, brought that part of the world into the living rooms and ateliers of twentieth-century Americans. There was no shortage of information to go on. Had he wanted to, Pissis could have easily and productively immersed himself in the contemporary literature and come up with a stained-glass window whose values were those of verisimilitude. But the California artist purposely chose another course, situating his account of Moses at Mount Sinai within an immediately recognizable and familiar American landscape—one calculated to appeal to the members of Congregation Sherith Israel and to heighten their sense of belonging. If ever there was a visual declaration of American Jewry's commitment to the New World, this was it.

To those who sat in the pews of this proudly modern sanctuary, everything about Pissis's representation—from Moses's having successfully scaled the nation's most formidable rock face to his presenting the Ten Commandments to the American people—not only made perfect sense but also seemed as natural, as organic, as could be. It is a measure of how far these American Jews had come in internalizing the notion that the Ten Commandments were an American phenomenon and in relishing their identity as Americans that this particular retelling did not occasion any waves. Situating Moses squarely within the context of the New World was entirely consistent with the congregation's decision to recite "America," rather than a Jewish composition, at the conclusion of the consecration of its synagogue's new building and to take to heart the following prayer: "May our country be an inspiration to us and next to God, may the highest praise be sounded to America—our country." Way back in 1850, the congregants of Anshi Chesed might not have been entirely sure where they stood; a half century later, the members of Congregation Sherith Israel harbored no such doubts. Like their stained-glass window, they too were deeply and unequivocally rooted in America.[14]

As it happened, Mother Nature had other plans for the good citizens of San Francisco, leveling much of the city in the earthquake of 1906. But the window, and the synagogue that contained it, miraculously survived to tell the tale of how Americans came to stand at the foot of Mount Sinai.

In the years that followed, American Jews from coast to coast made even more of the Ten Commandments. Casting them in metal and stone, as well as in glass, they relocated the twin tablets from the sanctuary's interior to the synagogue's exterior, where they loomed large and tall as the public face of American Jewry. A sculptural element in their own right, close kin to the monumental artworks that adorned the lobbies of sleek, postwar corporations and Miami Beach hotels alike, extravagantly scaled versions of the Ten Commandments increasingly graced the hundreds of Jewish houses of worship erected during the building boom in postwar suburban America. Synagogues were hardly the only religious institutions to benefit from the nation's changing topography. Churches also grew like topseed. "There's never been anything like it," observed the National Council of Churches in 1952, pointing to an estimated billion dollars' worth of construction projects within Protestant circles alone. Catholics, in turn, were averaging nearly four new edifices a week. Some attributed the latest expression of ecclesiastical vitality to insecurity and fear; others to interreligious competition, or what one observer likened to the "technique of denominational display"; and still others to a search for cohesion. Traveling the country for three months in 1954, journalist Barbara Ward and her husband found telltale proof of a national religious revival. "We did not need the evidence of polls or church attendance to confirm what we could so easily observe—the walls of new churches rising in the towns and countryside wherever we went," she wrote. "This revival of church-going," the journalist concluded, "can help to revive the social fabric of our overgrown society. . . . When neighbor meets neighbor within the loyalty of his religious faith, he strengthens a bond which no government, no state, no political authority can break."[15]

Amid this show of neighborliness, the Ten Commandments blossomed. In Arcadia, California, an eight-foot statue of Moses and the Ten Commandments adorned the exterior of the Foothill Jewish Temple-Center, while at Temple B'nai Israel of Aurora, Illinois, a free-standing "sculptured monument" of the Decalogue took pride of place on the lawn. In Portland, Oregon, Congregation Neveh Shalom boasted a towering set of Ten Commandments that looked for all the world as if it had been imported from a Hollywood movie set. Visible from the air, it guided pilots to a safe landing at Portland International Airport, or so it was said. (Americans seemed to like their Decalogues big and mighty. On the East Coast, in Fields of the Woods in Murphy, North Carolina, an earthenworks version of the Ten Commandments fashioned out of grass was reportedly so gigantic that it too could be seen from the heavens.) Meanwhile, back on Earth in suburban Chevy Chase, Maryland, a large-scale silhouette of the twin tablets greeted motorists as they drove past Congregation Ohr Kodesh's decidedly contemporary, low-lying building. Sprung loose from their traditional moorings, these visual expressions of the Ten Commandments, wrought from bronze, copper, metallic wire, and stone, were what we today would call "statement pieces." Scale was as central to their integrity as shape had been for their older counterparts.[16]

Prewar synagogues were immediately recognizable as Jewish houses of worship; their bulbous shape, majestic presence, and use of Jewish stars as exterior decorative features announced the building's distinctive identity even from afar. Not so the postwar suburban congregation, whose unornamented, concrete surfaces; stark, clean lines; and subtle presence did not immediately bring to mind a Jewish institution. It could just as easily have passed for a corporate headquarters, or, in several instances, even for a church. To avoid that possibility, the need for some kind of visual intervention or cue—a Jewish star, a menorah, or the two tablets of the law—became an architectural and cultural imperative.

Invariably, the members of the all-powerful building committee and the architects they consulted (and fired in quick succession) suggested some variation on Moses and the Ten Commandments. For the exterior of its brand-new building in northwest Washington, DC, architects presented Congregation Adas Israel with the option of reproducing the "famous Rembrandt painting of Moses holding the Ten Commandments" and casting it in "bold relief" in the form of a metallic plaque on the synagogue's front wall. When, in January 1949, a plaster version was presented to the building committee for vetting, its members voted down the proposition. The minutes of the meeting record that the "concensus [*sic*] of opinion was definitely against its use, as a result of which the following motion was made and passed: 'That the character and design of the plaque to be placed on the front wall of the new Synagogue building be left to the decision and discretion of the Building Committee.'" The disgruntled congregants at Adas Israel, as tight-lipped as their coreligionists nearly a hundred years earlier, supplied no reason for giving Rembrandt's depiction of the Ten Commandments the heave-ho.[17]

Unlike their predecessors, though, they did leave a modest paper trail. In the wake of this January meeting, the congregation's executive director, Abe Shefferman, was charged with getting in touch with the "Synagogue Architecture Department" of the United Synagogue of America "as to the propriety of a design of this kind." The fate of the congregation's Ten Commandments, it seemed, still hung in the balance; not everyone at Adas Israel was prepared to let them go. "[Your letter] poses an interesting question," responded Rabbi Albert I. Gordon, the organization's executive director, indicating that, given its importance, he would prefer

In postwar America, the Ten Commandments loomed large, as they did on the exterior of Congregation Neveh Shalom in Portland, Oregon. An avatar of the Judeo-Christian heritage, they were hard to miss. *Oregon Jewish Museum and Center for Holocaust Education*

to bring the matter to the Committee on Jewish Law and Standards, the Conservative movement's authoritative rabbinic body, rather than the lay-dominated group on synagogue design. The usual delays ensued, generating a show of tempered impatience on Mr. Shefferman's part. "Anything new?" he wrote to Rabbi Gordon at February's close. "The Building Committee and architects are to meet within the next few days and any information which you may give us will not only be appreciated but will help us a great deal in our final decision." Another few weeks would pass before the building committee received its answer: a resounding, unanimous no.[18]

Basing its decision on internal Jewish considerations rather than on aesthetic ones, the Committee on Jewish Law and Standards ruled that "there is the danger of people giving undue reverence to the figure of Moses. In Judaism, there has always been the reticence of allowing the man to be made central. It is the idea, not the man, embodying it, that is central in our tradition." Placing the "painting," as the committee mistakenly referred to it throughout, on the front wall of the synagogue was simply not acceptable. On the other hand, were the "painting" to be placed "anywhere else where it would have only a decorative value," that would be permissible. "It goes without saying," the ruling concluded, that "there would be no objection" if Adas Israel selected the latter form of display. The logic and language of this rabbinic response is puzzling, at least at first. Why was a representation of Moses and the Ten Commandments acceptable in one context but not in another? Was it kosher or not?[19]

What the rabbis were trying to say was that to single out and to isolate Moses and his Ten Commandments constituted an exercise in decontextualization, an act that came a bit too close for comfort to equating him with Jesus. On the other hand, if Moses and his Ten Commandments were placed in context, within the body of the synagogue, and as one element among many, the risks of that happening were minimal. In the company of others, Moses would not be misunderstood. The rabbis had a point. Still, the way in which they couched their decision was reminiscent of the yes-and-no response received by the congregants of Anshi Chesed in 1850. Equally opaque, this 1949 decision was not as helpful as the members of the building committee had hoped it would be. And so, rather than embroil themselves in any further complications, they decided to move on by forgoing Moses and his Ten Commandments in favor of an "heroic-sized" menorah incised on, and one with, the synagogue's stone facade.[20]

Adas Israel may have rejected the notion of an externalized Ten Commandments, but elsewhere throughout the country, American Jews roundly endorsed it, along with other modernist elements of design. "There seems to be little doubt that a majority [of congregants] have approved of most of the art," observed William Schack in 1955, referring to the highly stylized, streamlined sensibility of the postwar synagogue whose ritual furniture and artifacts, lighting fixtures, wall hangings, and Decalogues were nothing if not up to date. "That there is a minority which doubts and dislikes it is not surprising—the surprising thing is that it is so small." Even within their ranks, the critic continued, there was every reason to hope that "once the art is finished and in place, the will to believe it is good spreads from building committee to the rest of the congregation; approached in that spirit, with misgivings held in abeyance and dispelled by a good press, the art had time to work."[21]

He was right about that. Postwar depictions of the Ten Commandments "worked." They had panache. They also had staying power. They appealed. That so many postwar American Jews, or, more to the point, their representatives on the building committee, chose the two tablets of the law to flag the Jewishness of their most public facility speaks volumes about the ongoing resonance of the ancient text. Simultaneously Jewish *and* Christian, the Ten Commandments fit right in. "Now we meet in living rooms, public schools, zoning boards, in countless community endeavors, to the profit of intergroup life and at the expense of ethnic and religious boundaries," observed Martin E. Marty of suburban interactions between Jews and Christians. The fluidity, the boundary-crossing nature, of the Ten Commandments rendered it the perfect symbol of commonality. At a time when "Tolerance Trios," composed of a priest, a minister, and a rabbi, routinely made the rounds, preaching the virtues of religious tolerance and spreading the gospel of the Judeo-Christian tradition, enabling the idea to hit its stride—a time when Will Herberg's manifesto of America's "cultural oneness," *Protestant-Catholic-Jew: An Essay in Religious Sociology*, made the bestseller list—the Ten Commandments served handily as its visual companion.[22]

Writing in 1955, Herberg made a compelling case for defining Judaism, Catholicism, and Protestantism as three equal components of a distinctly American sensibility. He put it this way: "For all its wide variety of regional, ethnic, and other differences, America today may be conceived, as it is indeed conceived by most Americans, as one great community divided into three big sub-communities religiously defined, all equally American in their identification with the American Way of Life." And this way: Protestantism, Catholicism, and Judaism are "three diverse representations of the same 'spiritual values,' the 'spiritual values' American democracy is presumed to stand for." That each of the three faith traditions valued the Ten Commandments proved his point, highlighting what they had in common and bringing them closer to one another—and into the fold. Their widespread use by American Jews of the 1950s and early 1960s was no accident. In affixing the two tablets to the synagogue's exterior, where they functioned much like an oversized mezuzah, or better yet, as a giant exclamation point—we belong!—the synagogue declared itself as much an American institution as the meetinghouse or the parish church, a place where Judaism and Americanism came together as a unified whole. A deliberate visual strategy, the prominent positioning of the Ten Commandments defined Jewish space in familiar American terms, even as it celebrated, once again, the transformation of this age-old covenant into the stuff of common ground.[23]

All this, from America's embrace of the Ten Commandments to the multiple forms in which they appeared, would have been lost on Rabbi Isaac Leeser of Philadelphia, who in 1850 called on his fellow American Jews to "leave Judaism its outward dress." In a sweeping denunciation of contemporary attempts in antebellum America to "unjudaize Judaism," to rid it of its distinctive ways, he insisted that "outward dress becomes [Judaism] well, and tends to impress on the minds of its followers that it has a strength of its own, and a power of resistance to amalgamation, which has preserved it so long amidst the ruin of all things springing from the earth." Trifling with and "improving" the traditional form and setting of the Ten Commandments, in contrast, was a very bad idea, the road to ruination. American Jews would end up paying too high a price were they to abandon the tried and true in favor of more modern forms of expression, he warned. Nothing good would come of expanding the frame, the "outward dress," that contained the Ten Commandments. But Leeser's coreligionists, as well as those who followed in his wake, saw things differently. Setting in motion a process that began, tentatively enough, in the 1850s and that culminated, robustly and affirmatively, a century later, in the 1950s, American Jews imagined, and called into being, a much larger role for the Ten Commandments, one that acknowledged and saluted the twin panels of their identity.[24]

Chapter Four

Special Effects

New Yorkers of the 1920s were not easily dazzled. It took a lot to stop them in their tracks. Yet even the most hardened and world weary among them must have gulped and gaped when, on a wintry December afternoon in 1923, an oversized Moses, measuring four stories tall, was seen sailing down the Great White Way, holding on to the two tablets of the law as if his life depended on it. Those who missed him could be consoled by making their way to the corner of 43rd Street and Broadway, where an even more majestic, if stationary, version of the biblical hero held court amid a wondrous display of electric lights: Moses the lawgiver had become the stuff of a billboard. Reportedly the biggest sign ever hoisted in Times Square, it was said to have consumed more electricity than any of its electrified counterparts in the world. Moses "holds a gigantic stone tablet in his arms and looks with wondering gaze on the shifting multitudes below," related an enraptured eyewitness, adding that the "multitudes stare back their wonderment."[1]

Both the peripatetic and the illuminated versions of Moses were on hand to promote Cecil B. DeMille's brand-new motion picture, *The Ten Commandments*. Everything about it—the clever promotional gambits, the scale and expense of the production, the ambition of its director—was over the top, a testament to the man known as the "Hollywood Zeus." By the time *The Ten Commandments* opened in New York and Los Angeles to rave reviews, those who had avidly followed the gossip of "cinemaland" knew that it had cost a whopping $1.5 million to produce;

that its set on the sands of Guadalupe, California, was the largest ever built; and that it featured a cast of thousands, including three thousand animals—among them camels, horses, mules, goats, and guinea hens—all of whom had to endure extreme weather conditions that were nothing short of biblical.[2]

Even its beginnings were highly unusual. Most films of the 1920s owed their origins to a novel or a play, to the vision of the director or the whims of a Hollywood star. But this one grew out of a contest in which would-be participants, culled from the general public, were asked to come up with a compelling answer to the question "What is the most vital modern problem suitable for picturizing?" The winner would take home a hefty $1,000 in prize money for his or her suggestion. With the exception of the employees of the *Los Angeles Times*, which supervised the contest, and those associated with Famous Players-Lasky Corporation, whose Paramount Pictures bankrolled it, the event was open to anyone "who can hold a pen," limit his or her ideas to three hundred words, and write them, or preferably type them, on one side of a single piece of paper. "Boil down your hunch into the fewest possible words," contestants were told. And then "reboil."[3]

Submissions, often as many as fourteen hundred a day, flooded the Paramount mailroom, their "postmarks as varied as America itself. Erudite Boston, cosmopolitan New York, diplomatic Washington" made their voices heard, as did the residents of Mexico and Europe. Between the time the contest began, on October 4, 1922, and its conclusion a few weeks later, at midnight on October 31, thirty thousand ideas awaited DeMille and his staff. A photograph shows them dwarfed by heaps of paper: a bonanza of potential screenplay material. Cutting a big swath geographically, contestants hailed from all walks of life and included lawyers, doctors, socialites, a "sturdy little boy" of nine, soap manufacturers, and insurance agents. Their suggestions were just as varied as their biographies. One contestant suggested that a film about water would make for a thumping good yarn; another commended a film about exercise, insisting that it was the stuff of "great drama, romance, and thrills"; a third raised the possibility of a motion picture that focused on bridge construction. None of these ideas passed muster with DeMille. What won the day, his heart, and the prize money was the notion of a decidedly contemporary film about the Ten Commandments, an idea presented by at least eight contestants and hinted at by hundreds more. The people "want something big, something gripping and something elevating as part of their motion-picture diet," responded DeMille, explaining his selection. "They've never been given the Ten Commandments and they're anxious for it." Notwithstanding the Hollywood hyperbole and his disingenuous use of history, the filmmaker knew he was onto something. The Ten Commandments, he declared, were indispensable, much like "essential vitamines."[4]

Even so, DeMille's choice to make a film on a biblical theme was disappointing, at least at first blush. Some of the other propositions, even those that had to do with bridges or water, seemed much more promising, up to date, and imaginative. In comparison, a motion picture inspired by the Bible and its characters was, well, rather old hat, even ho-hum. For years, filmmakers had trained their sights and their cameras on Cain and Abel, on Noah and his Ark, and on the Passion of the Christ, hoping to erase the stigma that adhered to the new medium. Louche, sinful, and devilish, the movies, it was said—largely by the nation's churchmen—were simply up to no good. To prove their critics wrong, concerned filmmakers sought to "raise the motion picture out of the commonplace," elevating their product by associating it with the Bible.[5]

Soon enough, by the first decade of the twentieth century, growing numbers of clergy and religious educators began to see the merits of the movies, or at least those that made much of the Bible and related religious themes, and relaxed their opposition. Pleasing to the eye and to the ear, moving pictures were better than even the most eloquent homily, they grudgingly conceded, even going so far as to liken the medium to a potential "moving picture sermon" and film directors to preachers. Some went further still, identifying the movies as the latest in a long line of visual devices that uplifted the spirit, allowing how "a moving picture machine and a few thousand feet of film will do more good in the world than a beautiful window stained with all the tints that artists love to dream." In these and other statements that appeared repeatedly in the press, motion pictures increasingly received the approval of the church and its related institutions. As one YMCA official, a former critic-turned-convert, put it, referring obliquely to the movies, "I think we make a mistake to let the devil have a monopoly on so many of the good things."[6]

If the Vitagraph Company of America had its way, Satan would no longer stand a chance. In 1909, devoting its considerable "vitagraphic art and skill" to the making of biblical films, the company retained the services of Madison C. Peters, the "eminent New York divine," to write, produce, and direct motion pictures. Peters was well qualified; his bona fides encompassed archaeology and literature, the Holy Land of biblical times and the Holy Land of the twentieth century. Under his tutelage, Vitagraph's series began with the story of Moses, the "liberator and lawgiver of his race," whose popularity in the United States was second only to that of Jesus. *The Life of Moses*, company executives believed, would make for a wonderful motion picture, a "Biblical Film de Luxe," that called for the "skill of the magician," as well as the talents of the "historian, the archeologist, the artist, the skilled mechanic, the scientist and the editor." How could it miss?[7]

Through a series of five reels that Vitagraph released, one by one, over the course of several weeks, whipping up enthusiasm along the way, the highlights of Moses's career unfolded on the silver screen. "You dare not miss one of them," insisted the company as it serially staged Moses's encounter with the burning bush and re-created the ten plagues, the Exodus, the crossing of the Red Sea, the churning deaths of the Egyptians, and Moses's meeting with God atop Mount Sinai. Women, orientalized to the nth degree, bore jugs on their loosely clad shoulders and moved sinuously through space. Their heavily bearded menfolk were given to looking up toward the heavens and beseeching the Almighty. Both men and women gesticulated madly throughout the entire motion picture, while, now and again, tinted film stock that ranged from golden hued to bright magenta enhanced their movements.[8]

Some of the film's scenes were filmed indoors, on stage sets whose design either took their cue from the artistry of Gustav Doré and other celebrated illustrators of the Bible or reflected the latest archaeological finds, the "best of modern conceptions of life and customs in that ancient world." Other scenes, such as the crossing of the Red Sea, were filmed outside: in Brooklyn. "A dozen ways were tried to do it—mechanical, scenic and otherwise—until it was decided nothing but a real sea of water would suffice and get it across to the audience," observed one participant. Added a second, who had a small paid role as one of the Children of Israel, the "wilderness was down at Brighton Beach, and that's a mighty cold place for barelegged Israelites in January. We had to roll up our trousers so they wouldn't show under the costumes and the sandals they gave us in place of shoes and the stage paint tan we put on our legs wasn't much protection" against the elements. Still, concluded this aspiring actor, when it came to making a buck during the winter, pretending to be an Israelite sure beat shoveling snow.[9]

Despite the film's best efforts at naturalism, some critics were quick to cavil. *The Life of Moses*, claimed the owner of a small-town movie theater, wielding a long string of laments, was too stingy with its use of chariots, while its decision to have the camera zero in on the face of the characters "robs the audience of the spectacular efforts which should be so prominent in this class of work." And Moses's beard, he churlishly added, appeared to have been fashioned out of cotton. In fact, the entire production, from start to finish, seemed to him far too stagey and fake. Vitagraph's officials, having taken great pains to be as realistic as possible, were left scratching their heads. The only reasonable explanation they could come up with was that this particular member of the audience had positioned himself much too close to the screen.[10]

No matter where they sat or the religious beliefs they carried into the theater, most audiences were both excited by the film and mindful of its potential to bring together people of different faiths, if only for a few hours in a darkened auditorium. "The picture, while particularly interesting to the Jew, has an equal attractiveness for the Christian," acknowledged the Right Reverend Peters in an interview with *Film Index,* a contemporary magazine that chronicled goings-on within the industry, highlighting its broad appeal. That this journal heralded *The Life of Moses* as a "specially fitting LENTEN ENTERTAINMENT" and that hundreds of churches across the nation followed suit by screening the film for their congregants on successive Sundays preceding Easter suggest Peters was right, as did Vitagraph's repeated boasts of receiving "words of praise from all parts of the country." There "can be no question that the series is proving to be the greatest event of its kind in motion pictures since the Passion Play," it proudly noted.[11]

America's Jews, in turn, also took the film especially to heart— if on their own terms; comparisons with the Passion Play did not carry much weight in their circles. What endeared *The Life of Moses* to them was their emotional investment in Moses and the Israelites. From their perspective, the drama that played out in reel after reel was no fairy tale; it was their story. "The very appearance of Moses on the canvas is signal for wild applause that often continues for several minutes," observed the manager of the Milo, a movie theater in Minneapolis, whose patrons included large numbers of recently arrived Jewish immigrants. "As if completely in the dark as to the ending, the spectators watch with eager eyes. They follow the old story which seems never to become less thrilling in the telling. They always cheer the children of Israel on and when the Jews have passed safely through and the waters envelop their enemy, a mighty burst of applause breaks forth." Simultaneously enchanted and sustained, suspended midway between make-believe and belief, audiences at the Milo and at movie houses throughout the nation felt "almost as though present with the Hebrews," as one eyewitness would have it. The immediacy of the experience inspired them to pronounce the Bible "more real" than ever.[12]

Years later, the prospect or, more precisely still, the continued aesthetic and moral challenges of making the Bible seem even more real to increasingly sophisticated moviegoers of the 1920s fired DeMille's imagination, encouraging him to tackle this most evergreen of subjects. By then, the nation had fought a world war, the Roaring Twenties with its devil-may-care attitude toward discipline and ritual was in full swing, and Hollywood had come into its own, an arsenal of special effects at its disposal. Circumstances converged to make a brand-new film about the Ten Commandments unusually timely, even exigent. Egyptomania was in the air, a consequence of the public's fascination with the recent discovery of Tut-ankh-Amen's tomb, whose assemblage of glorious objects made the fabled riches of Ali Baba's cave resemble a "trinket shop in comparison." It behooved the filmmaker to seize the moment, to make "excellent hay while the sun still shines upon Egypt," and to capitalize on its current appeal by creating a film in which ancient Egypt had a starring role. With one eye on the box office and the other on movie magic, DeMille set out to produce a film about the Ten Commandments that would be unlike anything the American public had ever experienced, the "biggest picture ever made."[13]

But first: a screenplay or, in the parlance of the time, a "photoplay." DeMille immediately turned to Jeanie Macpherson, offering her what contemporaries described as the "biggest writing assignment ever handed out in motion pictures." A longtime "citizen of celluloidia," she had enjoyed a brief stint as an actress before spending the balance of her career as a screenwriter in close cahoots (some would say a bit too close) with the Hollywood director. For several months, Macpherson cast about for a device that would translate three hundred words into film footage and propel the ancient Ten Commandments into the "terms of modern, every-day life, with modern, every-day people." It was not easy to build a story around the Decalogue, she later acknowledged, noting that the resulting effort often left her in a "mental haze." Unable to find her way into the material, to transcend its association with Sunday school, the "scenarist" consulted with leading experts in the field of biblical studies and read hundreds of books, only to come up empty-handed. "I went far afield in my hunt for plot and situation, with increasingly unreal and artificial results," Macpherson wrote. The process was "bumpy. It started and stopped, ran and limped." Eventually, her fog lifted. Working at home one evening, she recalled, "I turned about entirely and began to drop plot and just think about life itself. . . . And the interesting thing that hit me was how easily and frequently human beings break all Ten Commandments."[14]

Once Macpherson had her hook, she quickly came up with a concept that divided the film into two parts, a "prologue" and the main story. Shuttling between the ancient Near East and modern-day America, between the "far-away time" when the Ten Commandments first entered onto the stage of history and the familiar present, where, more often than not, they were honored in the breach, its structure took the form of both a grand biblical epic and a small-bore drama. Macpherson's imaginative treatment, a "double-header" of a script, had the Ten Commandments, and those under its sway, leap across huge bands of time, cross the ocean, and careen between spectacle and domesticity—and all within the compass of two hours. Her action-packed screenplay played with space too, at times massing thousands of people in a single shot and at other moments zooming in on a single individual. As DeMille's screenwriter envisioned it, the first five reels of the film would focus on the historic relationship between the ancient Egyptians and the enslaved Israelites, culminating in God giving the Ten Commandments to Moses at Mount Sinai as his people gave themselves up to the golden calf. The balance of the film would then focus on the contemporary travails of a modern

Christian family, the McTavishes, whose members—one of them a carpenter—variously honored, blithely disregarded, or wantonly violated its tenets.[15]

Ambitiously conceived, the place where "the East and the West do meet," *The Ten Commandments* had something for everyone: the film was calculated to appeal. For those moviegoers who liked their moving pictures big and bold, DeMille's production ran true to form; those whose tastes ran to more intimately scaled dramas were also generously accommodated. Those who were fans of religiously oriented films would find much to admire, as would those who went to the movies to be entertained rather than inspired. An exercise in both history and sociology, this version of *The Ten Commandments* rooted for ancient Israelites *and* latter-day Americans, enclosing every one of its characters within a narrative that was nothing if not symmetrical, much like the twin tablets themselves. The story Macpherson and DeMille eagerly wanted to tell had both dimension and personality.[16]

No expense was spared in the telling. Everything *The Life of Moses* did well and to great effect, from its pursuit of verisimilitude to its sensitivity to the magical properties of color, *The Ten Commandments* did one better, ratcheting up its production values to an "undreamed of sumptuousness." So grand, so "gargantuan" in scale was DeMille's film that it completely eclipsed the earlier production, rendering it a historical curiosity, a footnote. From here on out, when Americans of the interwar era spoke of encountering Moses and the Ten Commandments at the movies, they had only the Paramount production in mind. You cannot blame them. Consider the differences between the Vitagraph and Paramount films, differences that arose out of DeMille's extravagant imagination on the one hand and the enhanced capacity of "shadowland" on the other. As the *Los Angeles Times* observed at the time, there is a "new Jupiter hurling bolts," and his name was DeMille. All he had to do was to push a dozen pearl buttons attached to a small wooden board—his very own "push-button storm board"—and twelve huge wind machines were set in motion. "Making storms to order used to denominate a great Greek god, 'The Thundermaker,' because of his reputed prowess in handling the elements," the paper went on to explain, "but nowadays thanks to modern invention, almost any well-equipped motion-picture director could give Jupiter cards and spades."[17]

On the wings of Greek mythology, DeMille could also raise an entire city, let alone a storm. Where Vitagraph made do with simply filming outdoors, on the shores of Brighton Beach, Brooklyn, DeMille, together with his designer, Paul Iribe, fashioned an immense set, the size of two football fields, in which ancient Egypt was re-created amid the sand dunes of Guadalupe, California. Replete with towering statues of mighty pharaohs and gigantic sphinxes, the film's physical ambiance was so convincingly detailed that more than one moviegoer insisted that the "Biblical story literally lives." It also left audiences slack-jawed. Said to be the "most colossal set ever constructed for a motion picture," its grand avenue and towering gates dazzled the eye and filled the mind with statistics. Here are some of them:

> Five hundred and fifty thousand feet of lumber, three hundred tons of plaster, twenty-three thousand pounds of nails, and seventy-five miles of cable and wire were used to construct the City of Ramses.
>
> One hundred tons of plaster and fifteen tons of modeling clay were used to build Pharoah's likeness.
>
> Thirty-three thousand yards—or nearly sixteen miles—of cloth were used to fashion three thousand costumes.
>
> Two hundred pounds of safety pins were used to secure the costumes.[18]

Harnessing the very latest technologies of enchantment, as well as tons of materiel to produce a series of "eye-smiting shots," the Paramount production went far beyond its Vitagraph predecessor

A monument to Hollywood, as well as to ancient Egypt, the colossal set of *The Ten Commandments* was made possible by an army of carpenters, painters, and builders. *Cecil B. DeMille Photograph Collection of the Margaret Herrick Library, Academy of Motion Picture Arts & Sciences*

in other ways as well. Where in 1910 *The Life of Moses* made limited, though inventive, use of color, *The Ten Commandments* saturated an entire scene, that of the Exodus, in the "exquisite" blues and reds of early Technicolor. Where in 1910, a single file of Egyptian chariots pursued the fleeing Israelites, hundreds now raced along the sand, flooding the screen and filling the eye. "Not since the legions of Rome were in the height of their glory have so many chariots been required," audiences were duly informed. As these two-wheel devices rushed, pell-mell, toward the viewer and at great speed too, like a runaway train, some of the charioteers actually tumbled from their seats, lifting excited viewers from theirs. And if that wasn't enough to keep audiences at a fever pitch, the scene of the Israelites crossing a "swirling, seething" Red Sea was a veritable "marvel," a dazzling display of movie magic.[19]

When asked at the time how he accomplished this, DeMille refused to tell, preferring to keep trade secrets to himself. Simultaneously courting an extreme case of hubris, he related how the Red Sea had been parted once before in history and that doing so a second time was "almost literally asking for a miracle. But it was done." The 1920s parting of the Red Sea, though, was not the result of divine intervention so much as the inspired handiwork of imaginative, if unsung, movie hands from Paramount's department of special effects who, taking a quivering mass of gelatin, melted it under the impress of scores of gas jets. When it came asunder, two cameras were at the ready. Subsequently, this piece of film footage

With its cast of thousands, DeMille's 1923 reenactment of the Exodus filled the screen and dazzled the eye, thrilling moviegoers across the country. *MSS P 146; Cecil B. DeMille Photographs, ca. 1900s–1950s; Photographic Archives, L. Tom Perry Special Collections, Harold B. Lee Library, Brigham Young University*

was "then reversed and shots of the Israelites crossing dry land and of Egyptians getting engulfed were double exposed on this scene." And with that, one of the legendary scenes in American film history had its day.[20]

DeMille could have stopped there, but he pressed on in his efforts to make *The Ten Commandments* a cinematic tour de force. The scene in which Moses received the Ten Commandments was another commanding moment, a thrilling admixture of science fiction and legend, technology and tradition. The biblical account has rays of light emanating from Moses's head. DeMille's account transformed them into electricity.

All alone on the craggiest of mountaintops, the lawgiver is visited by cathodes of electric light that shimmer briefly in the sky before exploding, like fireworks, into a cascade of familiar phrases. "There has been nothing on film so utterly impressive as the thundering and belching forth of one commandment after another," related the *New York Times,* a tad indelicately, as enraptured audiences, unable to contain their delight, cheered and wildly applauded yet another instance of the film's "vast pyrotechnic display." (Some, however, thought the cheering was less a matter of special effects and more a matter of taste. "It sounded like a popularity contest. 'Thou Shall Not Steal' didn't get much of a hand," an astute eyewitness related.) Even the decidedly humdrum moments of the film, like those that depicted the McTavishes in turmoil, were not without their quotient of "splendid thrill and dash." In one scene, the scaffolding of a grand San Francisco cathedral, built on the cheap by the villainous son who thumbs his nose at the Ten Commandments every chance he gets, comes crashing down upon his mother, killing her. In another, he meets his deserved fate, thrashing about in a small motorboat (*Defiance* was its not-so-subtle name) amid giant waves that would soon engulf him, much as the Red Sea of yore had engulfed the ancient Egyptians. In these and other heart-wrenching scenes, the second half of the film went far beyond the "details of Balzacian fidelity," as one literate observer would have it, to awaken the senses and stimulate the moral imagination.[21]

At nearly every turn, sound both complemented and heightened the visual excitement of the silver screen. Under the baton of Hugo Reisenfeld, the film's impassioned musical director, kettle drums boomed and organ pipes rumbled, reproducing the sounds of thunder. Iron cauldrons, filled to the brim with birdshot, manufactured the "swish" of the all-consuming waves while the "quivering, crashing, resounding blare" of the strings and the wind instruments kept audiences on edge. At some climactic moments, Reisenfeld drew on his own compositions, at other moments he made use of Bruckner, and at still other key points, the score represented the "combined efforts of Rimsky-Korsakov and Reisenfeld." Whatever its source, the film's acoustic landscape demanded much of its musicians, who, finding it all a bit too "strenuous," demanded a double shift—and overtime pay.[22]

For all its aural and technical sophistication, the film's greatest coup de théâtre resided in its use of extras. *The Life of Moses* drew on a small assembly of "barelegged Israelites," local actors all. Its successor mobilized several hundred recently arrived Jewish immigrants to play the beleaguered slaves. As DeMille would later explain in his autobiography, the decision to deploy them added a level of historicity and a depth of emotionality to the screen that could not be manufactured. "Both in appearance and in their deep feeling of the significance of the Exodus, they would give the best possible performance as the Children of Israel," he declared. Inclined to see these newcomers as "types" rather than as individuals, DeMille and his "efficient" casting director insisted they were the closest thing to the ancient Israelites. "They *were* the Children of Israel. This was their Exodus, their liberation." Reducing the traumas of Jewish history to a series of dramatic gestures, DeMille had no qualms about employing Eastern European Jews as extras, especially since he believed they did not require much by way of direction. "Their wonderfully expressive faces shone with the holy light of freedom as they followed Moses [i.e., Theodore Roberts] toward the Promised Land," the filmmaker subsequently, and grandiloquently, related, intimating that he had had nothing to do with their performance; acting the part came naturally to them. That may be. Still, DeMille was not above laying things on a bit thick and egging everyone on by playing a full-throttled version of the Largo from Dvorak's *New World Symphony* to heighten their emotions as they poured out of Ramses's immense urban gates and made for the sea. It worked. As Theodore Roberts, who played Moses, recalled, participating in this scene was an "intense emotional experience I can never forget."[23]

Those who are constantly on guard against essentializing and other forms of stereotyping may find DeMille's strategic use of immigrant Jews somewhat distasteful. Contemporary accounts, though, make it abundantly clear that these latter-day Israelites were complicit—at one with DeMille—in assuming their new-found screen identity and in making it seem as if nothing stood between them and several thousand years of history. "To these Jews," observed Hallett Abend of the *Los Angeles Times*, who visited the set, the "making of the film was not business and not work. It was almost a reality—a transmigration to biblical times." His impression was confirmed by others. The "scenes in the sands of Guadalupe were not merely a make-believe to them; they were a natural expression of a race memory," observed Rita Kissin, referring to her coreligionists. Among the twenty-five hundred members of DeMille's cast of thousands, she too had been on the set when the Exodus was filmed, an eyewitness to the naturalness of the acting. "No need to tell them how to register fear and despair, how to shrink from the whip, how to plead for mercy," she related, praising their collective performance for its truthfulness.[24]

Kissin may have spoken in level terms of authenticity and the *Los Angeles Times* in highfalutin terms of transmigration, but those who inhabited the role had an even more immediate connection to the Exodus. We do not even have to think of Egypt, chimed in one of their number, explaining his motivation. Our experience is also one of "liberation, with America as the Promised Land." Curious as to whether all of the immigrant extras felt the same way, conflating the biblical tale of deliverance with its modern-day counterpart—redemption through immigration—Kissin queried them about their decision to leave their newly established homes, brave lacerating winds, endure burning hot sands, and suffer a lack of kosher food (a situation that, to his credit, DeMille immediately remedied by building and equipping a kosher kitchen), just for a bit part in a movie. The money sure came in handy, responded one of their number, a female extra. Even so, she would have worked for nothing. "It's just like living in dem times when we got the Thora—and now we're going to get it all over again in a picture by Mr. DeMille."²⁵

Did this anonymous extra, a recent transplant from Eastern Europe, truly believe she was going to receive the Torah once again—and from the hands of a man more commonly associated with Greek gods than with biblical prophets? Was this film extra so enraptured by DeMille and under the spell of the movies or so intoxicated by her newfound freedom that she really saw herself at Sinai? While her English may not have been up to snuff and her sense of American geography and culture may have been a bit thin, it is unlikely that she was all that gullible or, for that matter, had fallen prey to Hollywood hoopla. Nor was she talking out of her hat, exaggerating every step of the way for the benefit of the press and in the spirit of the very best of American boosters. No, this Eastern European immigrant-cum-actor meant what she said, but she said it while under the influence of simulation, a powerful emotional state that evokes empathy and stimulates identification. Re-enactments of historical events, be they the Exodus from Egypt or the Civil War, power their participants by collapsing the categories of time and space, enabling them to feel as if they were there: literally on the scene. What with the sand and the sea, the throngs of

half-clad coreligionists, the thrill of the hunt, and the thrum of the *
music, this Exodus seemed every bit as real as the first one.

Simulation was also the key to the film's success, the reason
moviegoers responded so fully—and physically—to its two hours
plus of running time. They did not use that word, of course. They
spoke, more simply, of the real and the literal. Audiences at the
George M. Cohan Theater in New York or Grauman's Hollywood-
Egyptian Theater in Los Angeles did not just cheer, stomp their
feet, applaud like mad, or feel as if propelled from their seats at peak
moments in the movie's progression of scenes. They went further
still, referring repeatedly to having been transported while watching the film, "transported in the sense that we feel actual participants of the migratory movement of the Israelites and suffer and
sympathize with them." Like the Eastern European immigrant
extras, though at a remove of several degrees, audiences too experienced a profound sense of immediacy, of being there. The movies,
with their bells and whistles, made that possible: spectacle played
midwife to history. When *The Ten Commandments* first debuted,
Will Rogers famously quipped that he did not expect it to have
much of a run. "I'm afraid it'll never be popular—because nobody
has read the book." He was right about that. Many Americans then,
as now, fumbled their way through the Decalogue, unable to recite
all ten prescriptions or mixing up the order in which they appear.
But the humorist was wrong about the film's success: it went on to
enjoy a record run at the nation's leading movie theaters, drawing
a half million viewers in New York City alone within the space of
six months.[26]

Americans of the 1920s knew enough to know that the Ten
Commandments mattered. The film reminded them why. By setting this foundational text within a recognizably human context,
by rendering it accessible, as only motion pictures could do, the
movie brought home its importance. "For centuries, the story of
Israel has lain frozen in hieroglyphics, manuscripts and books. In
the sunlight of modern invention it has thawed into something

colorful, something dramatic, something real," gushed one of the film's many fans, referring, of course, to the power of the movies. Mixing his adjectives like mad, he was onto something. Film dissolved distinctions; it allowed for both possibility and accessibility. Another member of the public—Joseph Silverman, the rabbi of New York's prestigious Temple Emanu-El—had a similar experience. Having been on the movie set where he "relived the Exodus in 1923," he recalled how the film had a great effect on him. For years Rabbi Silverman had taught and studied the Ten Commandments, but never, said he, "have I been so profoundly impressed as during the hours when I was privileged to see the reproduction of this great code in terms of living and breathing humans."[27]

Amid the public's chorus of hosannas, critics lavished praise on DeMille, tripping over one another in their eagerness to come up with the most mighty and encompassing of superlatives: colossal, epic, stupendous, gorgeous, magnificent, a "cinemasterpiece," and, "at last, a superpicture!" This is one movie "that you cannot, by any stretch of the imagination, afford to miss," gushed one admirer, while another maintained that it put paid to, once and for all, the notion that photoplays were bad for you. The Ten Commandments "will last as long as the film on which it is recorded. It wipes the slate clean of charges of any immoral influence against the screen."[28]

Admittedly, some of the film's more literal-minded critics experienced a spot of trouble with the manner in which the biblical tale dissolved abruptly into a tale of modern times, moving with absolutely no warning from writhing Israelites at an orgy presided over by the golden calf to an elderly woman peeling potatoes in her drab and humble kitchen. Still other critics had reservations about the movie's entire second half, not just its introductory scene. Following on the heels of the thrill-a-minute prologue, they found the second part of the film, its modern sequence, rather tame, even lumbering in comparison, and were not shy about letting DeMille know that they thought it a real letdown, an "anti-climax." The film "goes from the sublime to the ridiculous," lamented a critic from the *New York Times*. "It is too much like an elaborate leather binding on a dime novel." Building on that theme, others found even the intertitles something of a disappointment. "After the spacious Scriptural lines, with their sonorous King James English, echoing the even more spacious ancient Hebrew, there was a distinct drop into Mr. Mencken's language," wryly observed a critic from the *Telegram*, pointing out the ordinary speech that accompanied the modern-day story.[29]

DeMille met his critics head-on. The decision to follow the spectacular with the domestic was not an easy one, he publicly admitted, confessing that it gave him a couple of sleepless nights. But, ultimately, he believed it to be the right decision, an "inspirational stroke of genius" on Macpherson's part, heightening the contrast and sharpening the mood between the biblical and the contemporary sections of the film. "The transition from the glittering spectacle of Hebraic and Egyptian hosts to a simple, modern home was exactly like a blow between the eyes," DeMille explained, proud of the way its visceral impact "banished any form of tedium," while also making clear to contemporary audiences why and how the Ten Commandments continued to matter. "All the spectacle that went into the beginning would not have been worth the film required to record it . . . had it not influenced the thought and action of the characters," the filmmaker explained at considerable length—and often. "Spectacle, for spectacle's sake, is not only not worth what it costs, but it can be a positive detriment if it is not hooked up with human action." In this instance, the movement from one era to the next was an act of "translating the message of ancient days into understanding modern situations."[30]

In the face of DeMille's frequent and elaborate justifications, some critics stood their ground and continued to insist that the film's second half was no match for its first. A majority, though, ended up seeing things DeMille's way and came to savor the film as an integrated whole, as did the moviegoing public. Audiences may have come for the biblical part of the proceedings, but they stayed in their seats until the lights came up.

Perhaps they were drawn to the actors, a "galaxy of headliners recruited from the Paramount lot," and captivated by their "attention arresting" skills. Their names—Rod La Rocque, Estelle Taylor, Theodore Roberts, Leatrice Joy, Nita Naldi—may no longer mean much to us. But contemporary audiences knew who they were and relished the ways in which these popular performers either inhabited their customary roles or expanded upon them. Nita Naldi, for instance, parlayed her reputation as an "adventuress" by playing Sally Lunn, the sexy Eurasian who brings down the logos-breaking Dan McTavish, while the veteran theater actor Theodore Roberts dispensed with his customary cigar long enough to give a haunting performance as Moses. Although he acknowledged more than his share of "ordeals" while working on the film, having "suffered keenly in the chilly blasts whilst guiding the people across the wind-swept bed of the Red Sea," portraying the biblical hero turned out to be the "most inspiring work of his career," or so he said.[31]

Meanwhile, Rod La Rocque, "one of Hollywood's most eligible bachelors ("But he's no boulevardier. No fop"), came into his own thanks to the film, playing the evil son while also managing to arouse and hold on to the audience's sympathy, no mean feat apparently. On the strength of his performance, La Rocque was "suddenly forged into the vanguard of movie men most talked about. He has excited consuming curiosity among women." Despite La Rocque's star turn and the blossoming of his sex appeal, *The Ten Commandments* was not really about him or his costars. Though the actors made a point of collecting a newspaper clipping every time the press singled them out for praise, and pasting it into a scrapbook thick with plaudits, they had to know that they played second fiddle to the film's pageantry and spectacle. After all, "it was the mass that counted, the magnificence of the temples and palaces and the grandeur of the natural scenes," not their actorly chops.[32]

Capitalizing on its visual splendor, advertisers had a field day with the film. They touted it as a must-see and, in language riddled with exclamation marks, breathlessly invoked its memorable scenery! Its cast of thousands! Its glorious costumes! Mere "words cannot describe Cecil B. De Mille's *The Ten Commandments*," gushed Grauman's Hollywood Egyptian Theater, devoting an entire page in the *Los Angeles Times* to doing just that. Between the theater's neo-Egyptian décor, with its "Cleopatra fore-court," and the film itself, "Do you wonder [why] we say it is like attending a world's fair? If there was a world's fair in Los Angeles, surely you wouldn't miss it."[33]

American Jewish audiences had even more of an incentive to see the film. While most broadsides underscored the film's exoticism and allure, those that appeared in Jewish venues, from newspapers to synagogue bulletins, trumpeted its historicity. "Moses! Sinai and the Tables of the Law! Ramses, Pithon, Pharoah! Wilderness and the Golden Calf! Slaves and Taskmasters! Idols and Adonoi! Footsore Wanderers and Charioteers! And in the background and to the fore, the Ten Words!" bellowed *The Truth*, the weekly publication of Temple Beth Emeth of Flatbush, Brooklyn. Not to be outdone, a generously proportioned advertisement in the *American Hebrew*, bearing the headline "The Ten Commandments—After 2448 years," insisted that the "motion picture camera and projection machine bring to us for the first time adequate pictorial representation of Israel's Exodus from Egypt." Lest anyone miss the point, the text then proceeded to catalog the film's virtues, its fidelity to the biblical narrative. Thanks to DeMille's virtuosity,

We now see on the screen
- the flight of our nation from Egypt
- the parting of the Red Sea at the command of Moses
- the Decalogue thundered from the clouds onto the mountain-side
- Moses receiving the Ten Commandments from the Lord.

At once a cherished memento and a compendium of information, souvenir booklets like this one transformed moviegoers into fans. *Warshaw Collection of Business Americana—Motion Pictures, Archives Center, National Museum of American History, Smithsonian Institution*

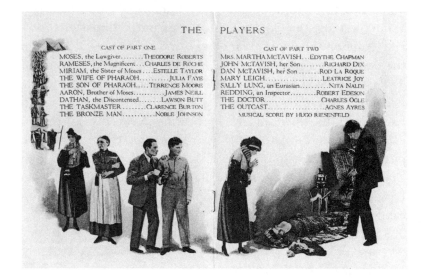

It adds up to the "world's greatest message combined with the world's greatest melodramatic entertainment now playing twice daily." Another advertisement put things more effectively and succinctly still. Drawing on the biblical designation for the ancient

Hebrews, it roundly declared that *The Ten Commandments* "was made to order for Israel," for the Jewish people. No ifs, ands, or buts about it.[34]

Had *The Ten Commandments* come to a full stop at the end of the fifth reel, this display of cultural assertion would have been entirely appropriate. But the film not only continued to unspool for another six reels, tantamount to an additional hour of screen time, but also placed a Christian family at its center. And yet, none of the Jewish publications, including numerous Yiddish- and English-language Jewish newspapers, commented on that rather stunning and abrupt shift in focus. More puzzling by far was the absence of any mention of one of the film's most powerful closing frames—a parting shot of a long-haired Jesus, bathed in light, seated in a manger. Admittedly, his back was to the audience. All the same, there was no mistaking his presence and the symbolism that sustained it; the accompanying intertitle, "Lord—if thou wilst—make me clean," made certain of that.

Let us say you shut your eyes for a few seconds and missed that scene; what of the rest of the film? Even if you were prepared to concede that the flickering image of Jesus was more of a grace note than a substantive element of the movie, how to account for the presence of a Christian family at its core? No member of the audience, Christian or Jew, wide awake or dozing, could possibly mistake the McTavishes for beleaguered Israelites, let alone Eastern European immigrant Jewish extras or contemporary American Jews. How, then, to reconcile American Jewry's proud insistence that the film was made expressly for them with its explicit and unwavering Christological sensibility? It is almost as if the Jews in the audience sat through the first five reels and then left en masse before the sixth was underway. The secular press made no mention of Jesus either, only deepening the puzzle. Would that have spoiled the ending, robbing it of its element of surprise? Did Paramount's public relations machine insist on silence? Is it possible that some audiences were treated to a print of the film that left out the scene with Jesus?[35]

Moviegoers, especially those who had read all about the film in the Jewish press before seeing it, must have been thrown for a loop. Filling the George M. Cohan Theatre, they had to wonder: what happened to Moses? And yet, in lieu of brickbats, demurrals, or, at the very least, a raised eyebrow or two, there was complete and utter silence within the Jewish community. A few years later, when DeMille released *King of Kings,* a film that depicted Jesus's crucifixion, all hell had broken loose. The American Jewish community then mustered its considerable reserves in loud, angry, and sustained protest at what it took to be a most unfavorable and unflattering portrait of the Jews. But not this time. In December 1923 and during the first few months of 1924, the American Jewish community rallied around *The Ten Commandments* as if it were its own, playing down the film's Christian overtones and playing up its Judaic sensibility. It was not just that they felt praised by *The Ten Commandments* and pilloried by *King of Kings.* Embracing one film and rejecting another had more to do with the community's willingness to cede the Ten Commandments to the American people.

In an early adumbration of that grand proposition, the Judeo-Christian tradition, America's Jews drew a straight line from Moses to Jesus, choosing to emphasize what they held in common and ignoring what they did not. Casting the Ten Commandments in the form of a shared heritage made it possible to think in those terms, enabling them to turn a blind eye to the rest of it. They had ample precedent, after all. Building on the example of the ancient relic of the Ten Commandments buried deep within American soil or the stained-glass window that situated Moses in California, *The Ten Commandments* was just the latest, and arguably the most potent and splashy, of long-standing efforts to reclassify the covenant between God and the Israelites as a covenant between God and the American people. What's more, in its formulation of a "Prologue," followed by a contemporary story, the structure of *The Ten Commandments* echoed America's construction of its own history: first, the biblical prologue—of subjection, Exodus, resettlement, and nation building—and then its recapitulation and culmination, thousands of years later, in the new Promised Land of America. This congenial reading of history cast the Israelites in a leading role, enabling their latter-day descendants to feel at home in America, to see themselves as progenitors of the national narrative rather than as interlopers or johnny-come-latelies. It is little wonder, then, that Jewish audiences were quick to define the film as the "epic story of a birth of a nation," a description that cut both ways, entwining the destiny of one with the destiny of the other.[36]

America's Jews were not the only ones to link the two gestational narratives. "Here is a superb dramatic picture of a great community movement," observed the *Telegram*, comparing *The Ten Commandments* with *Covered Wagon*, another one of DeMille's creations. "The progress of the Israelites out of the land of Egypt, out of the House of Bondage, is an even nobler story than that of the American pioneers moving westward as told in the *Covered Wagon*." Jeanie Macpherson was even more resolute in asserting a firm and unassailable connection between the ancient story and its modern-day counterpart. As she put pen to paper to come up with the framing device that would transform the Ten Commandments from a rhetorical conceit into a cinematic one, she wrote: "It is the fame of Moses . . . to have waged a peregrinatory campaign that built a Nation—the laws of States—in a sense, Civilization itself! If one may compare the sacred with the profane, the labors of Moses may be likened to those of our heroic covered wagoners of the 1843–49 period who traversed thousands of miles of desert and wilderness in order to break ground for new communities on the Pacific shore." Moses was nothing less than "the first of the Pioneers!" By dint of such weighty and inspiriting comparisons, *The Ten Commandments* would go on to enjoy long lines of satisfied customers. As its creator told the readers of the *Ladies' Home Journal*, aiming high, movies like this one "will make for unity and for a certain great one-ness in the world. Ultimately, it may even be one-ness with God."[37]

Chapter Five

Take Two

Every spring since the 1970s, Americans have taken to their televisions to watch the unspooling of *The Ten Commandments*, the second of Cecil B. DeMille's films to grapple with the biblical text. Hard as it is to imagine, it is an even grander affair than its predecessor. When the $13.5 million film, at the time "the biggest motion picture project on record," debuted in 1956, critics and moviegoers alike hailed it as "stupendous, eye-filling and magnificently decked out." Pointing to its "assortment of dancing girls, notables like Moses, Joshua, and a brace of Pharoahs," *The New Yorker*, its tongue firmly planted in its cheek, trumpeted the film's legion of actors, its "cast of millions, or what seems to be a cast of millions." Since then, in what has become a holiday tradition, an annual occasion, all its own, households across the country tune in to ABC, or to one of its many affiliates, on the Sunday that falls midway between Passover and Easter for the lavishly staged, nearly four-hour-long broadcast. Whether you are Christian or Jewish, a regular worshipper or a reluctant one, you know these two springtime holidays are right around the corner when TV listings herald the film's appearance.[1]

The yearly showing of *The Ten Commandments* does not just mark time. Like all rituals, it puts audiences in a proper frame of mind, preparing them to receive Easter and Passover with the right mix of awe, reverence, and understanding. With its wide-angled, ecumenical perspective on biblical history, the film also celebrates the relationship between faith and freedom, rendering them as indivisible and as American as apple pie. As the *New York Times* critic Vincent Canby once observed, *The Ten Commandments* is nothing if not a form of Americana. Some households even return to *The Ten Commandments* year after year to refresh their familiarity with the biblical narrative before they attend religious services or conduct a Passover Seder. Still others go even further, integrating portions of the film into their reading of the Seder's primary text, the Haggadah. "I always rent the flick for my annual Passover seder. I pop the tape in the VCR, cue it up to the plagues and we watch them in Technicolor while we're reading that section of the Haggadah," one celebrant recently explained, giving new meaning both to improvisation and intertextuality.[2]

The publication in Israel of a pint-sized version of the Haggadah called *HaHaggadah Sheli* (My Haggadah) generously illustrated with color stills from *The Ten Commandments* goes hand in hand with the way in which contemporary Jews have translated the film into a ritual gesture. No bootleg version, the use of this visual material was authorized by Paramount Pictures Corporation. Perfectly keyed to the text, color stills punctuate the age-old narrative at precisely the right moment; someone—an editor, an art director, perhaps even a publicist—knew what he or she was doing. When, for instance, the enslaved Israelites are mentioned, an adjacent page contains a scene from the film in which half-clad slaves, pulling on a rope, were brutalized. When the Haggadah discusses the ten plagues, it is accompanied by the movie moment when the waters turned blood red before Pharoah's astonished eyes while a mighty Moses looked on. The crossing of the Red Sea, a penultimate scene in the film, similarly assumes pride of place as the volume's centerfold. The small scale of the book—you can hold it in the palm of your hand—indicates that it was probably intended for children. That its visual enhancements are drawn, and derive their authority, from Hollywood rather than the Holy Land also suggests a youthful audience in search of immediate connection.[3]

A curious amalgam of antiquity and contemporaneity, of tradition and make-believe, *HaHaggadah Sheli* is a prime example of that old saw about bringing coals to Newcastle, or, as its Hebrew equivalent would have it, hieroglyphics to Egypt. Better yet, if you are inclined to think theoretically rather than expressively, the text might put you in mind of what academics like to call mediation and re-mediation: the movement of a word, image, or thought across multiple genres and layers of interpretation so that, as in the game of "Telephone," it ends up as something else again. Itself but not itself. Something curious is afoot here. Few major motion pictures enjoy an afterlife, much less remain actively, even ingeniously, in circulation long after their initial debut. But the postwar version of *The Ten Commandments* keeps on ticking, even though its visual conventions and dialogue increasingly strike many viewers as dated, downright risible, and even "high camp." What is it about this film that renders it evergreen? Is it a matter of scale? Of visual extravagance? Does the "muscular arrogance" of its handsome Moses, an effective counterweight to most images of the lawgiver in which he is typically depicted as heavily bearded and overbur- dened, have something to do with its long-standing appeal? Or is the film's longevity bound up with its very American message of deliverance, redemption, and the promise of perfectibility?[4]

Cecil B. DeMille attributed the success of *The Ten Commandments* to all these elements—plus one. The film, he explained whenever he could, was a testament to the power of democracy and the impera- tives of brotherhood. Whether speaking to a band of studio execu- tives, addressing an audience of moviegoers, or appearing before the Pacific Southwest branch of the National Women's League for Conservative Judaism to receive its annual Torah Award, the leg- endary filmmaker, by then in his seventies, emphasized the Ten Commandments as common ground. Although he stopped short of invoking the "Judeo-Christian tradition" per se—that phrase had not yet become a popular rhetorical bellwether—he understood the Decalogue to be the source of freedom and insisted that the "Magna Carta, the Constitution of the United States, the Declaration of Independence, all came from Mount Sinai."[5]

COPYRIGHTED, 1901 BY PROVIDENCE LITH. CO.

THE TEN COMMANDMENTS.—DUTIES TO GOD.

Ex. 20 : 1-11.

GOLDEN TEXT :—Thou shalt love the Lord thy God with all thy heart.

Luke 10 : 27.

Thanks to the handiwork of the Providence Lithograph Company, early twentieth-century Americans encountered Mount Sinai in the form of pocket-sized Scripture cards. Later generations encountered Mount Sinai on a much grander scale—at the movies. *Warshaw Collection of Business Americana—Religion, Archives Center, National Museum of American History, Smithsonian Institution*

Contemporary concerns, very much of the moment, fueled DeMille's determination to produce a second movie on the subject. "I feel there never has been a better time to restate the Ten Commandments," he told a reporter from the *American Examiner* on the eve of the film's debut. On other occasions, the man dubbed "Mr. Movies" liked to boast that *The Ten Commandments* was "as modern as this morning's newspaper," blurring the line between his production and the original one. DeMille's homage, clarified Bosley Crowther, the *New York Times* film critic at the time of its release, was "weighed with responsibilities." Some of those responsibilities had to do with picking up the pieces, with restoring moral order, in the wake of a devastating world war. "Today, after more wars and rumors of wars, the world stands on the brink of complete annihilation. Only under the Ten Commandments can men live together," DeMille maintained. His film was also intended as a stern rebuke to Communism. These days, he told yet another interviewer in 1958, there were many places in the world where God was denied and people were treated as state property. *The Ten Commandments* offered a "way out." It "shows that man is a free soul under God. . . . That has been the great battle since Moses and Pharoah started fighting it, and it is the greatest battle today since Russia and the United States are continuing the battle."[6]

Some have even argued that the Holocaust cast a long shadow on the production. "You cannot see the DeMille epic without being reminded that it came out when memories of the Holocaust were fresh," observed journalist Steven R. Weisman in 1998. Writing a few years earlier, Henry Wilcoxon, one of DeMille's longtime lieutenants and the associate producer of *The Ten Commandments*, went ever further, intimating that his boss's decision to return a second time to the Ten Commandments was his way of making amends to the Jewish people in the immediate aftermath of their wholesale extirpation. Wilcoxon recounts how DeMille's plans to make another film about the biblical covenant were initially greeted with derision. "You must be joking, C.B.!" Barney

Balaban, then president of Paramount, was reported to have said. "That's the most ludicrous thing I've ever heard of!" As Balaban's dismay spread throughout the room, threatening to undo C. B.'s project, as well as his dignity, Adolph Zukor rose to his longtime colleague's defense. "I find it embarrassing and deplorable that it takes a Gentile like Cecil here to consistently remind us Jews of our heritage! What do you have to argue with, gentlemen? After we have just lived through a horrible war where our people were systematically executed, we have a man who makes a film praising the Jewish people. . . . We should get down on our knees and say 'Thank you.'"[7]

We have only Wilcoxon's word that this really happened, but it is utterly plausible that it did, at least in some fashion. This was not the first time that I came across a connection between DeMille's motion picture and the Holocaust. Once, following a speech I gave about the film in Montgomery, Alabama, a woman in the audience—a friend of a friend of Charlton Heston's—approached me to say that she knew "for a fact" that the actor had the destruction of European Jewry very much on his mind when he inhabited the role of Moses.

Whatever DeMille's rationale or that of his stars, he devoted considerable attention to the movie. Ten years in the planning and five years in the making, *The Ten Commandments* gave new meaning to "epic." A colossal undertaking from start to finish, the "statistically intimidating production" was said to have employed fifteen thousand people at a time, among them "hordes of extras," many of them local Egyptians passing as ancient Israelites. An extensive collection of four-legged creatures, "menageries of camels and other animals," rounded out the "mighty" cast." *The New Yorker* even suggested that the production encompassed more living things than the entire population of Moses's Egypt.[8]

To his many laurels as producer and director, field marshal, and animal wrangler, DeMille could now add that of biographer. Where the 1923 film focused on the meaning of the Ten Commandments, this one focused on Moses, tracking him, and his moral awakening, from a "baby in a basket" on through his callow youth and his emergence as a hero. So intense, so single-minded was the film's interest in Moses that a number of critics suggested the film would have been better off, and certainly more honest, had it been called by its rightful name: Moses, or the Prince of Egypt, rather than *The Ten Commandments*. But that was not to be. From DeMille's perspective, the lawgiver and the law were one. The arc of his life could not be understood apart from the covenant in which it culminated. It is little wonder, then, that the filmmaker selected Charlton Heston to play Moses. A latter-day Adonis, his physical muscularity reinforced the pull, the muscle, of the Ten Commandments.[9]

Not just any old biopic, the 1956 film drew on scale, pyrotechnics, and history to comment on, and deepen, the immense hold that the biblical figure and, with him, the Exodus and the giving of the Ten Commandments already had on the American imagination. The immensity of the production was enough to compel Americans to take a second look. "People, beasts, pageantry, scenery, costumes, jewelry tumble at you as from a cornucopia," exclaimed Father James Fenlon Finley, all a-twitter at the sixteen sphinxes and towering arches, some reaching as high as one hundred feet, that lined the way to Pharoah's court. Arguably the largest construction project in Egypt since the Suez Canal, the newly fashioned Egyptian city outside of Luxor even boasted its own trio of pyramids.[10]

"Obviously, DeMille was thinking big," related a visitor to the set, with considerable understatement. And that was just the half of it. The star-studded cast added to the razzle-dazzle. A who's who of stage and screen, it featured Yul Brynner, Vincent Price, Sir Cedric Hardwicke, Edward G. Robinson, and Dame Judith Anderson, who, as the doleful Memnet, was the "possessor of ominous secrets." Chewing the scenery, the cast also filmed several of its scenes "on location," where, amid the vast expanse of the desert and the stony, arid, seemingly immutable landscape, that expression accrued a new meaning. "We rolled our cameras from Goshen to the Red Sea—then across the wilderness of Shur, down through the wilderness of Sin and up the steep, barren, majestic, awe-inspiring slopes of Mount Sinai to the holy ground where Moses stood to receive the law," DeMille animatedly recounted, as if he had personally experienced the Exodus from Egypt.[11]

Back home on the Paramount lot, the filmmaker and his crew upped the ante by making use of the latest technology, from "glowing" Technicolor to the singular talents of the studio's special effects department. Ensuring that "reds were never richer, blues never brighter and hues of lavender, pink and sienna bathed temple scenes in a kind of Florentine light"; simulating the crossing of the Red Sea by means of hydraulic equipment capable of spilling three hundred thousand gallons of water in "two minutes flat"; sonorizing the voice of God by recording and then slowing down an actor's words until they seemed like vibrations from some other world; heightening a sense of tension and foreboding by making use of the theremin, a spooky, ghostly-sounding electronic instrument with "invisible strings"; filling the screen with a sickly green vapor that put audiences in mind of radioactivity: all the tricks of the trade were deployed to animate the drama—the "greatest Cinderella story in the entire world"—that lay at the heart of the biblical account.[12]

Authenticity, the third and, arguably, the most fascinating element on which *The Ten Commandments* pivoted, allied scale and technology with history—or, more to the point, with the process of transmission. If in 1923 the film's authority was vested in its immigrant Jewish extras, this time around it rested on scholarship. "Cutting a vivid swath through the Old Testament country," DeMille brought Technicolor and VistaVision, Paramount's brand-new "large-screen process," to bear on the sacred writ and on other equally ancient writings, among them the works of Philo and Josephus, as well as the Midrash. The Midrash?! This was arguably the first, and possibly the last, time that Hollywood trained its sights on that age-old compilation of Jewish lore. We will never know for sure how DeMille, the son of a committed Episcopalian, first became aware of the existence of the Midrash, which was not exactly a household word in America in the 1950s. The filmmaker enjoyed having clergymen of various denominations on the set; perhaps one of them, a rabbi, in the course of casual conversation might have mentioned the Midrash as a potential source of lively detail and legend about the travails of Moses. DeMille also deployed an army of researchers and a team of clergy consultants, some of whom were described erroneously as "talmudic scholars." Their collective knowledge, and canvassing, of background material might have brought this collection of Jewish folktales and legends to light. One can only speculate. But clearly, something about it appealed to DeMille, so much so that, as the stately procession of movie credits unfurled, there it was: the Midrash, alongside the other ancient texts of Philo, Josephus, Eusebius, and the Holy Scriptures "in accordance" with which the film was made. American audiences, with the possible exception of those from New York, were no doubt puzzled by the Midrash's sudden burst of fame.[13]

A form of endorsement, a way to establish, and burnish, the film's credentials, DeMille's strategy of trotting out the Midrash was of a piece with his insistence that every aspect of *The Ten Commandments,* from its color palette to its sound, be as authentic, as historically true, and as rooted in the sources as possible. "You are to invent nothing out of your own talented imaginations," he charged his team of four screenwriters, prompting Aeneas MacKenzie, one of them, to observe that working on the picture was more akin to a "detective investigation than the composing of a screenplay." Accounting for gaps in the biblical account, where references to Moses were either scant in number or elliptical in tone, and reconciling them with contemporaneous Egyptian sources, where Moses was conspicuously absent, was no easy matter. It was not for want of trying.[14]

The efforts of DeMille's scenarists and researchers to fill in the blanks, to ensure that every single detail was "based on actuality or within probability of actuality," rather than on myth, led them to consult 950 books, 984 periodicals, 1,286 clippings, and 2,964 photographs. Acting on the belief that contemporary Bedouins were the closest one could come to the ancient Israelites—"modes of life do not change much in biblical deserts as centuries pass by in slow rhythm," it was said—they cast a searching eye on how the members of this nomadic culture built their tents and shepherded their flocks. Their wide-ranging and thorough research ultimately filled an entire book: *Moses and Egypt: The Documentation to the Motion Picture, 'The Ten Commandments,'* a publication of the University of Southern California Press. Then, as now, it was not uncommon for some kind of publication, a compilation of production notes or a series of film stills, to accompany the release of a major motion picture. But a nearly two-hundred-page book fueled by footnotes and published by an academic press? This was something else again.[15]

At first blush, the film's display of bibliographic extravagance paralleled its visual extravagance; the first read as an extension of the second: yet another form of showmanship. On closer reflection, the two made for strange bedfellows. Where feature films are typically an exercise of the imagination, nonfiction books are typically an exercise in scholarship. Fact and fancy do not usually go hand in hand. DeMille made sure they did, transforming history into a special effect every bit as dazzling, calculating, and audience pleasing as more traditional forms of cinematic wizardry. Not for nothing, history was placed front and center in the film's lengthy trailer, which was designed to grab the public's attention. "What a time we had with that trailer," recalled those who had worked on it. "Every word was turned over and over like a pearl." Shuttling between scenes set on the banks of the Nile and those set in a private study (possibly DeMille's own?) chock-a-block with props from the film, scads of artwork and piles of oversized books strewn just about everywhere, the mini-film featured "Mr. Movies" at his most avuncular. Carefully leafing through the pages of Philo, Josephus, and the Holy Scriptures, the film's preferred term for the Bible, he quoted at length from various passages and then, just as carefully, connected them to specific moments in the movie. One fed the other.[16]

The book DeMille commissioned went even deeper. A testament to his determination to adhere to a "standard of absolute authenticity," it too brandished chapter and verse. Under the direction of Henry S. Noerdlinger, DeMille's personal assistant-turned-"research consultant," the film's production team consulted everything: Egyptian wall paintings and biblical illustrations, nineteenth-century ordnance surveys of the Sinai Peninsula, and the latest archaeological discoveries from Qumran. Reading and rereading their Bible, as well as Buber and Freud, Breasted and Kenyon on Moses and the ancient Near East, they looked to these authoritative texts for information on how to build the film's sets, dress the actors, choreograph their movements, outfit their steeds, cross the Red Sea, and receive the Ten Commandments. No detail was too small or too ethnographic. What kinds of tents did the ancient Israelites inhabit? (Answer: "Those still in practical use among the tent-dwellers of Arabia and the wilderness of Sinai.") What kinds of colors did they fancy? (Answer: The tribe of Reuben was partial to red, the followers of Naphtali preferred wine-colored hues, while those who clustered under the banner of Benjamin liked "all colors combined.") How did Egyptians move? What kinds of musical instruments did they play? "Did they eat roast beef or lamb chops or what?"[17]

Not everyone hungered for this level of detail. Some, in fact, found the movie to be "suffocated in scholarship" and turned up their noses at the prospect of reckoning with the past, let alone with footnotes. Even DeMille admitted that "research does not sell tickets at the box office." But for those who fell somewhere in between—a tad curious about, but not entirely engaged by, the back story—a brightly colored, oversized booklet, approximately

twelve inches long and nine inches tall, provided a much more dis-
tilled and accessible entrée. In its handsome pages, colored litho-
graphs of scenes from the movie, the artistry of Arnold Friberg,
"one of the greatest interpreters of Biblical subjects," brought the
production to life, as did row after row of sharp black-and-white
photographs of its good-looking stars, along with their capsule
biographies. Designed to be a visual experience rather than a textual one, the pamphlet also featured several pages' worth of drawings that depicted, among other things, the shields wielded by the
Twelve Tribes, as well as a series of Egyptian cartouches and wall
paintings. It also boasted a representation of the twin tablets themselves, down to their putative Late Bronze Age, "Pre-Canaanite"
script, whose scrupulous reproduction—the contribution of
Professor Ralph Marcus of the University of Chicago's Oriental
Institute—was a matter of considerable pride.[18]

The most compelling aspect of the booklet, its most resolute
salute to history, was an ocher-colored map, drawn to scale, of the
"very ground where Moses trod more than 3,000 years ago": Upper
Egypt, Lower Egypt, the Wilderness of Shur, Mount Sinai. Richly
detailed, the document invited viewers to cast their eyes on the
"supposed route of the Israelites," and to follow in their footsteps as
if they were on a latter-day pilgrimage. The map's publication reinforced the film's relationship to the ancient Near East and, with it,
DeMille's pursuit of a pedigree. Despite the huge financial cost and
logistical nightmare that filming in Egypt entailed, he insisted on
it. The first time around, the filmmaker made do with the dunes of
Guadalupe. Not this time: "Moses came through the desert and so
did Chuck," DeMille categorically declared, conflating the biblical
hero with the actor who played him and situating the two of them,
quite literally, in the wilderness.[19]

Why did DeMille go to such great lengths to ensure the film's
authenticity, even publicly attributing his decision to cast "Chuck"
as Moses thanks to his "amazing" resemblance to Michelangelo's
Moses rather than to his gifts as an actor? Admittedly, this was

not the first time the cinemogul had made so much of verisimilitude. More than thirty years earlier, when working on the first *Ten Commandments*, DeMille had also publicly celebrated the production's relationship to reality, to the lived experience, to the honest, emotional behavior of his immigrant cast of extras as they left Egypt. But this time around, his claims of authenticity seemed louder, more frequent, more literal, even insistent.[20]

They were hard to fathom too, given the many instances in which the film took great liberties with history and "freely adapted" the biblical narrative. It is not just that DeMille preferred to build his own version of ancient Egypt rather than set his film against the backdrop of the ancient pyramids: they appeared to be too weathered, too ravaged, by the passage of time, he explained. (Some visitors to Egypt agreed with DeMille's assessment. These ancient edifices, related journalist William K. Zinsser, "are about 5,000 years old and they look it.") Yes, we can concede that DeMille had a point: from the perspective of his viewfinder, perhaps the pyramids would not hold up well enough on the silver screen. Securing permission from the Egyptian authorities to build a set from scratch than having to tread carefully—politically and logistically—on ancient and hallowed soil also made sense. Even so, how could DeMille and his publicists speak so easily of the film's Egyptian pedigree when it was more a matter of patina, of show, than of substance? And what of the film's invention of a romance between Moses, the prince of Egypt, and Nefretiri, the "Hereditary Princess of Egypt," or its decision to substitute some of the characters' biblical names for those his screenwriters made up? Hearing Moses's mother called Yochabel rather than Yocheved provided audiences with a consistently risible moment. The clotted dialogue of the love scenes at which, remarked one observer, even *"True Romance* might boggle" supplied another. How, then, to reconcile these latter-day interpretations and interpolations with DeMille's repeated expressions of fidelity to the Bible and to historical truth?[21]

Questions about the filmmaker's commitment to authenticity were first raised at the time of the picture's release. A coterie of disgruntled clergymen was quick to point fingers—to accuse him of artistic license, of having his way with the facts or, worse still, with deliberately obscuring the real meaning of the Bible. The "problem with DeMille," declared one aggrieved Boston cleric, "is not that he is too realistic but that he is not realistic enough." More strident, more incendiary by far, were the comments made by Tom F. Driver, a drama instructor at Union Theological Seminary, who heaped scorn on the film within the pages of the high-toned *Christian Century,* creating quite a flap within ecclesiastical circles. His argument was a simple, if impassioned, one: *The Ten Commandments* led good Christians astray. Its "star-studded cast, with thousands of supporting actors, whose very names seem to cause the screen to sag with the weight; the colossal length; the flaming Technicolor"—all the features of the film that won it plaudits, even among churchmen—did Christianity a disservice, Driver charged. "Dedicated to things external" rather than internal, to the material rather than the spiritual, these elements ran counter to the true spirit of the Bible, at once literalizing and corrupting it. Even the Almighty himself suffered at the hands of DeMille and his minions. "The DeMille God is imprisoned in the DeMille style, which means in the irrelevant minutiae of Egyptian culture and the costume director. He bears no resemblance to the Old Testament Lord of History." His indignation in full flower, Driver concluded his screed by drawing on a stunning use of literary parallelism. Urging the "people of the churches" to stay clear of *The Ten Commandments,* he called on them to reject the film "quite as absolutely as the god of the Golden Calf was rejected by Moses."[22]

Men of the cloth had no monopoly when it came to denouncing the film or lamenting how far it had fallen from the original. One of the fiercest and most unbridled condemnations came from the pen of Lillian Reznick Ott, a columnist for the *California Jewish Voice.*

In high dudgeon, she characterized *The Ten Commandments* as a "de-Biblicized, de-Hebrewized, be-DeMilleized, be-fictionalized Hollywood extravaganza of flim-flam and mishmash having as much to do with the Ten Commandments as a mongoose with a teal duck." Take that, DeMille! Less pungent but still packing a punch was a cartoon that also appeared in the *California Jewish Voice* in which a middle-aged couple was shown leaving a movie theater whose marquee bore the words "Now Playing the Ten Commandments." "It wasn't at all like the book," read the caption.[23]

DeMille not only rejected such characterizations of his work. He would not give an inch. From where he sat, high up on his special director's chair, his bullhorn at the ready, *The Ten Commandments* was awash in history, its commitment to the past unimpeachable. "Our constant thought while we were making 'The Ten Commandments' was: Can we be worthy of its theme? That demanded close adherence to the Bible and to the facts," the filmmaker piously explained off-screen. He did much the same thing on-screen as well, adding several minutes to the film's running time by indulging in the kind of special pleading that only a man of his years and stature could get away with. What came to be known as the "Prologue" to *The Ten Commandments* took the form of a monologue—or better yet, a manifesto. As the camera lingered on the details of a fringed theater curtain, the viewer heard a series of muffled footsteps. The curtain then parted, and a besuited DeMille suddenly appeared and, clutching a skinny pole of a microphone, spoke directly to the audience: "Ladies and gentlemen, young and old. This may seem an unusual procedure—speaking to you before the picture begins. But we have an unusual subject: the story of the birth of freedom, the story of Moses." He then went on in the most measured of tones to frame the film by talking (yet again) about its fidelity to history, as well as its topicality, drawing on language increasingly familiar to anyone who had followed the making of the film.[24]

A rhetorical gambit? A promotional tool designed to woo moviegoers at a time when film was fast losing ground to television? A way to face down critics so that "when wise guys make fun of the ballet in Seti I's court . . . C.B. calmly refers them to an ancient Egyptian mural which shows every movement to be authentic?" Yes and no. There was no question that DeMille and his team of publicists, thinking strategically about how best to promote the film, harnessed history and geography to public relations. Claims that *The Ten Commandments* "brings Sinai" to viewers back home and that "when you see the Red Sea, *it is* the Red Sea" were hard to beat, as was Adolph Zukor's sweeping assertion that "with the help of Cecil B. DeMille, we were there when the Lord handed Moses the Ten Commandments." It was also the case that DeMille unequivocally believed that his beloved film stayed true to the facts and that what others might dub an act of interpretation was actually a way to fill in the lacunae in the historical record, not mess with them. The only concession he was prepared to make—and make it he did on national television—was to acknowledge that his interventions, such as they were, were best understood as translations, as part of a process of interpretation that deepened, rather than distracted from, the original text. "When people see the Bible retranslated through a 'living medium,'" he explained, "they receive a much stronger impression."[25]

Then again, America's "Number One Producer-Director" could not afford to get things wrong; fiddling with what he took to be the facts was not an option. The stakes were too high. "There is no place for the usual fiction in a picture that deals with the interpretations and circumstances from which not one—but three!—of the world's great religions have sprung," DeMille insisted. He might have added that, given the well-publicized advances in biblical archaeology since the interwar years, as well as increasing opportunities to tour the Middle East, American audiences were much better informed about that part of the world than they had ever been. Meanwhile, the eruption of the Suez Canal crisis, which had taken place only a few short weeks before the debut of *The Ten Commandments*, had once again thrust Egypt and Israel into the limelight. In what was an uncanny coincidence, a marvelous accident of timing, at least as far as Hollywood was concerned, the film made its debut "against the raw news of modern conflict between Egypt and Israel—a conflict," excitedly related one newspaper, "that has its preamble in the Book of Exodus."[26]

DeMille turned out to have been right. Audiences, for the most part, responded enthusiastically to the film's distinctive mix of history and hokum, of "scripture and spectacle," applauding, cheering, and at times engaging in seemingly strange behavior, especially when God's voice was heard repeatedly exhorting Moses to defy Pharoah, rally the troops, and lead his people out of Egypt and into the Promised Land. One of the film's representatives, on hand one fine day at a screening at New York's Criterion Theatre, heard "strange, clicking noises" in the auditorium, prompting him to check the film and the projector, as well as the sound equipment. Though he found nothing untoward, the noise persisted. It turns out that the clicking sound was the result of the female members of the audience snapping open and closing shut their purses as they rummaged for a hanky with which to dry their teary eyes.[27]

When not weepy, audience members, many of them dressed to the nines as if headed to church or synagogue, transformed what might have been an ordinary night at the movies into a grand occasion. Those who saw the film at the Criterion in New York, the RKO Grand in Boston, and any number of downtown movie palaces have said, time and again, that it was a "very big deal." The experience of sitting in a darkened theater with hundreds of others, eyes riveted to a screen that was filled, edge to edge, with Israelites in flight or with a close-up of Moses speaking to God atop Mount Sinai was itself a form of communion, possibly even an "adjunct and a comfort to faith." Even those who came just for the popcorn or the high jinks could not help being moved by the film, whose appeal ran deep. "The high and the mighty, the lowly and the meek," as well as those "not unanimously DeMille-minded," reported the *Motion Picture Herald*, were taken in by *The Ten Commandments*. Audiences of all stripes flooded movie theaters across the country. By one count, as many as 800 of them, including 365 drive-in theaters or "ozoners," as they were then called, featured the nearly four-hour film. In response to popular demand, it was shown twice a day during the week and as many as three times on Saturday. So well trafficked was *The Ten Commandments* that within a year of its debut, those who followed such things gleefully reported that the film had played to an estimated 21.9 million people and had grossed $26.5 million. *The Ten Commandments*, excitedly reported one observer, "is bringing in business by the carloads." Added another, "Paramount officials almost run out of zeros when they project its eventual earnings."[28]

It may come as no surprise to learn that large numbers of African American moviegoers were particularly enamored of the production. The presence on-screen of more than one hundred people of color—"tan beauties," they were called—and in important roles, like those of the king and queen of Ethiopia, was one source of its widespread appeal. Another, of course, was the film's call to freedom. Amid the cruel irony of watching *The Ten Commandments* in segregated theaters like the Royal and the Ashby in Atlanta and the Tivoli in Chicago, African American audiences resonated to its themes of deliverance and redemption. How could they not? This film is the "Voice of the Minorities crying to be heard," proclaimed Mrs. L. McAllister Scott in the *Atlanta Daily World*. "Take your family so that the story of struggle will never grow dim."[29]

America's Jews were also among the movie's biggest fans. Hailing *The Ten Commandments* as an "overwhelming motion picture experience," they closely followed stories of its production, featured interviews with DeMille in the pages of their newspapers, and delighted in pointing out that the demand for tickets was "unprecedented in theatrical annals," "phenomenal," and the stuff of "extraordinary acclaim." When not trafficking in

A blockbuster of postwar America, *The Ten Commandments* attracted a steady stream of paying customers eager to see for themselves what the fuss was all about. *MSS P 146; Cecil B. DeMille Photographs, ca. 1900s–1950s; Photographic Archives, L. Tom Perry Special Collections, Harold B. Lee Library, Brigham Young University*

hyperbole, Jewish newspapers throughout the country also made sure to inform their readers that in Cincinnati, say, the film had run for a record-breaking eighteen weeks, or that in Boston, it had closed after a whopping thirty-six weeks. Other newspapers, to be sure, did much the same thing. The runaway success of *The Ten Commandments* made for good copy. Writing in 1957 about the film's reception in African American circles, the *Chicago Daily Defender* noted that in the twenty-five-year history of the Tivoli Theater, "the south side showplace has enjoyed many successful film engagements but the volume of the past ten day period has never been equaled," while in Atlanta, the Ashby movie theater extended the film's run due to "unprecedented demands." Within the Jewish community, though, keeping tabs on the number of people who actually saw *The Ten Commandments* was more a matter of monitoring than of reporting.[30]

Repeated references to the success of the Paramount production furnished proof—a statistical assurance—that the story of the ancient Israelites and the heroism of Moses mattered to contemporary Americans, leaving them with a heightened understanding of Jewish history and a "greater respect for the People of the Book." Integrating the Jews into the body politic, *The Ten Commandments* scored high in what the Jewish Community Council of Metropolitan Boston called "community relations values." In projecting a dignified and moving image of the Jews as a morally and physically courageous people able to endure "untold hardship in the name of human liberty," *The Ten Commandments* was the best thing that happened to the Jews of America since, well, its predecessor some thirty years earlier.[31]

For all its reassuring box office success and the torrent of praise that accompanied it, the film's detractors were equally thick on the ground. Many outdid themselves in their efforts to knock DeMille's production off its pedestal; years later, their critique makes for very good reading, even a guffaw or two. Some, bridling at the movie's excessive length, beseeched DeMille "to let his people go." They also wondered if it was entirely possible that not one single piece of film had ended up on the cutting room floor. "Did the scissors get lost?" Still other naysayers thought *The Ten Commandments* was truer to Hollywood than to the Bible: "Hollywooden" was how one wit put it. Questioning the "improbable pulchritude" of its leading ladies and its rhythm of heavy breathing, they raised the possibility that the film might best be described as "Sexodus" rather than Exodus. Moses, in turn, came in for more than his fair share of zingers. "Charlton Heston is ludicrously miscast," his critics charged, putting paid to DeMille's notion of authenticity. He "looks less like a man who staggers into the desert to find God than one who flies into Palm Springs to freshen up his tan." Was nothing sacred?[32]

Even the film's much-vaunted special effects gave rise to a torrent of complaints. They do not hold a candle to those of the 1923 film, said some with long memories. Others, hewing to a much more recent perspective, damned the special effects as mechanical and even cheesy, more reminiscent of a B-grade, sci-fi flick than a first-rate production. A case in point: the finger of God as it wrote the Ten Commandments. Anything but commanding, it put some viewers more in mind of a rocket ship than a divine digit. God's voice fared no better than his finger. Unctuous rather than booming, as one might expect, it had more in common with a television announcer than a heavenly emanation, booed the critics. And, in what was perhaps the cruelest cut of all, a chorus of voices wanted to know if the "talmudic scholars" who had consulted on the film were now doing penance.[33]

Anticipating criticism, especially from conservative religious leaders—DeMille had been down this road many times before—he made a point of enlisting the public support of rabbis, priests, and ministers, whose hosannas he planted on billboards and advertisements, sometimes in lieu of and at other times alongside those of more typical blurbs from *Variety*. "We are not the same after we have lived through the experience of following Moses through this picture," said one clergyman. While his comment could be taken in any number of ways, those of his colleagues were less ambiguous and more surefooted. "It makes the Bible thrillingly alive," said another divine. Said a third commentator, a rabbi particularly heartened by its ecumenism, *The Ten Commandments* was a "stirring film. I was moved as Moses, conscious that the Law has its source in the one God of all men, conceived of it as the universal law." Perhaps the fullest vote of clerical confidence, one well worth quoting from at length, came from the pen of Bishop Gerald H. Kennedy of the Methodist Church of Los Angeles. Taking vigorous exception to those who, like the Union Theological Seminary instructor Tom Driver, decried *The Ten Commandments* as overly commercialized fluff, he applauded DeMille and his cinematic labors. Negative press like that of Professor Driver "makes it sound as if this film is the greatest adversary we have had to face since the Reformation." I don't see it that way, he chided. While there are several things I might change, I think *The Ten Commandments* is a "great film and will do a great deal of good. It brings back into the center of our thinking the truth that God is the foundation of freedom, it makes Moses alive and great. It has scenes which are unforgettable and moving. It seems to me that the church ought to be very grateful to Mr. DeMille and Paramount for making *The Ten Commandments*."[34]

Fans, both within and without the church, expressed their gratitude by showering DeMille with all manner of awards, among them the Paul Revere Trophy, a gift from the City of Boston, and a statuette of Michelangelo's Moses, a gift from the Cinema Lodge of B'nai B'rith. Although the most exalted of all prizes, an Academy Award for Best Picture, eluded him—*The Ten Commandments* received only one, for special effects—other forms of adulation came DeMille's way and from institutions as diverse as the Daughters of the American Revolution and the Women's League for Conservative Judaism. Rarely on the same page, these two disparate groups invoked similar language and sentiment as they extolled the virtues of the film and its maker, underscoring the extent to which *The Ten Commandments* was common ground in postwar America or, at the very least, an awfully big tent. Over and over again, in a steady refrain, DeMille was praised for his contributions in "advancing brotherhood," for "focusing the eyes and ears of the world on mankind's most magnificent moment," and for "exemplifying the richness of the American tradition," themes that, in the public mind, seemed increasingly interchangeable. The Hollywood mogul was often on hand to receive these accolades; he enjoyed the public acclaim. When unavailable, he sent Heston in his stead, which seemed to please those in attendance even more, especially if they happened to be women. At one such gathering, the sixty-sixth annual Continental Congress of the Daughters of the American Revolution, "gray-haired delegates and pretty young pages alike gave out audible sighs when [Heston] stepped on stage to receive an award," reported the *Washington Post and Times Herald* in 1957, adding that "three of the pages accompanied him in a taxicab to the airport."[35]

Some of those admiring fans might have sported a Ten Commandments charm bracelet, one of the many inventive and fast-selling promotional items that accompanied the film's release. Girls and their mothers could now dangle the Decalogue from their wrists. Fashioned out of an inexpensive silver alloy, the bracelet consisted of ten miniaturized tablets, each of which bore the text of a commandment. "Each and every one is guaranteed, will not tarnish, fade or corrode," the accompanying sales pitch declared with no apparent trace of irony, giving new meaning to the eternality of the biblical covenant. Others had the option of decorating their home or office rather than their person. They could place a miniaturized version of the twin tablets on their desks and hang on their walls a vividly colored poster of the film in which Moses, astride Mount Sinai, threatens to bring down the Ten Commandments— and the wrath of God—on everyone's head. Burying one's nose in an "ingenious," if not too taxing, crossword puzzle was yet another form of popular engagement: "2 Down: Land of Hebrew Bondage. 14 Across: One who joins the Exodus. 24 Across: Used after a prayer. 29 Down: How many commandments?"[36]

Paramount's publicity department and its field advertising division kept churning out stuff, hailing *The Ten Commandments* for having the "most amazing potential of any motion picture!" And American consumers kept accumulating it, eager to keep the Ten Commandments close at hand. If you were lucky enough to be among the many visitors to the Paramount lot while *The Ten Commandments* was being filmed—"statesmen, educators, members of the clergy, the military and the rank-and-file have paraded

Moses (Charlton Heston) listens in as two masters of the camera—photographer Yousuf Karsh (left) and filmmaker Cecil B. DeMille—discuss their art and craft. DeMille hired Karsh to make portrait photographs of the film's leading lights. *MSS P 146; Cecil B. DeMille Photographs, ca. 1900s–1950s; Photographic Archives, L. Tom Perry Special Collections, Harold B. Lee Library, Brigham Young University*

in goodly numbers through the Paramount gates," reported one of their number—you might have come away with your very own marble version of the twin tablets, a personal gift from DeMille. If not, *Ten Commandments* merchandise was available for sale during the film's intermission, at its conclusion, or, in the case of the charm bracelets, at selected jewelry and department stores. Where most giveaways were modest in tone and small in scale, other promotional items such as six-foot-tall stone monuments to the Ten Commandments were something else again. Dubbed "granite movie posters," they steadily graced the public square of more than one hundred American cities in the years since the film made its debut. They were no isolated venture or, for that matter, merely a self-serving, self-referential gesture. Rather, Ten Commandment monuments were of a piece and at one with the desire of individual Americans at the grass roots to possess the Ten Commandments, to wear them on their sleeve (or wrist), to be within close range of their sheltering presence.[37]

The twin tablets that Charlton Heston cradled in his arms, stone entablatures that DeMille insisted had been fashioned out of the red granite of Mount Sinai itself, enjoyed a happy afterlife too: for a spell, they came to rest in Brooklyn. An exhibition at the Brooklyn Public Library on biblical languages incorporated them into its display. "Although the original tablets are long since lost, these modern reproductions are a scholarly substitute," explained the exhibition's organizers, noting that the "South Canaanite lettering" had been "supplied" by the distinguished University of Chicago scholar Ralph Marcus. What an understatement! The celebrated philologist did a lot more than that. His involvement with DeMille began in 1953 when the two men met in the Windy City. In the course of their discussion, the professor sketched the ancient words of the Ten Commandments on a piece of cardboard so that the filmmaker could see what they might have looked like. A lovely detail, that: a marriage of the sublime and the utilitarian. Later still,

Marcus furnished DeMille's associate, Henry Noerdlinger, with a detailed memo that outlined how he had arrived at his conclusion that the "rather formal, but not excessively so" lettering of the Ten Commandments should assume the form of early Canaanite script. Both men, smitten by Marcus's rendering and the expertise that sustained it, would go on to make full use of it. (To his credit, DeMille made sure publicly to acknowledge the professor's contribution on—and off—the silver screen.)[38]

In the years that followed, Marcus continued periodically to field additional philological questions about the Late Bronze Age from Noerdlinger and others associated with the film and its marketing. In one instance, which seems to have tried the professor's patience, a jeweler preparing "ornaments" in connection with the film asked him to confirm that the script they contained was the correct one. In another, equally vexing inquiry, a member of Paramount's graphic arts department busily engaged in designing a "house," or a "cabinet," to hold the red granite tablets securely in place once they were no longer needed on the set wanted to be sure they were correctly positioned. "Mr. deMille [sic] has told us you are the foremost living scholar on the ancient Semitic languages," wrote A. F. Mendel in February 1955. "At your earliest convenience, will you kindly mark the attached drawing and return it to me." It is hard to say whether or not Marcus complied. But it is not hard to imagine that the distinguished professor felt a tad diminished, even aggrieved, by his connection to The Ten Commandments. Who can blame him? After all, when a lifetime of painstaking scholarship becomes fodder for popular consumption, a movie prop is transformed into a proof text for a library exhibition, and authenticity gives way to artifice, we have certainly come full circle, blurring the line between what is faux and what is real, between a simulation and the genuine article. DeMille would have relished the confusion. In our postmodern era, when everything is up for grabs, shouldn't we?[39]

Filmmaker Cecil B. DeMille proudly displays the two tablets of the law used in the film to the Reverend Billy Graham. DeMille placed much stock in, and derived considerable pleasure from, the scholarly authenticity of the biblical script he used to fashion the Ten Commandments. *MSS P. 146; Cecil B. DeMille Photographs, ca. 1900s–1950s; Photographic Archives, L. Tom Perry Special Collections, Harold B. Lee Library, Brigham Young University*

These days, you can discover all kinds of related Ten Commandments paraphernalia on eBay or at auction, from delicately colored costume sketches replete with swatches of fabric to an orange metallic pleated chiffon gown trimmed with metal lotus flowers at the hem, one of the many splendid garments worn by Anne Baxter in her capacity as Nefretiri. Several sets of lightweight, fiberglass versions of the twin tablets, the "Holy Grail of motion picture memorabilia," are also available for sale. One of these Decalogues bears a most telling inscription on its back or verso side, a series of words that serves as a most fitting coda. "Left and Right," it reads. The first time I came across that wonderful nugget I laughed out loud. I continue to find it funny the tenth time around—and hope you do too. Americans may lay claim to a Ten Commandments charm bracelet, own their very own copy of the film, and make a point of screening it annually. But when it comes to their moral compass, they still need directions.[40]

Conclusion

Pedigree

Sid Grauman, the owner of the eponymous Los Angeles movie palace, Grauman's Hollywood Egyptian Theater, could think of no better way to mark the 350th screening of *The Ten Commandments*, which was scheduled for late May 1924, than by pulling out all the stops. Roving musicians, zithers in hand, would welcome the guests as they made their way from the lavish, palm-strewn forecourt of his "cinema temple" into its sanctum sanctorum, a 1,760-seat auditorium. Once inside, they would be bowled over by its array of "special decorative features" designed to provide "added Egyptian atmosphere" to the already over-endowed facility. To top things off, every member of the audience would be given a gift, a party favor: a miniature replica of the Ten Commandments. Nothing could be more appropriate than these "little bronze tablets," Grauman proudly told the *Los Angeles Times*, as he contemplated the prospect of thousands of "Hollywood folk" returning home with the Ten Commandments tucked under their arm or stowed away in their purse.[1]

Some of us might sooner roll our eyes than applaud this "memento" from Grauman's Hollywood Egyptian Theater. Others might go further still, recoiling at the idea of a Decalogue cut down to size. But making light of or scowling at the notion of the Ten Commandments as a novelty item runs the risk of misreading the past, of mistaking one generation's relationship to the Ten Commandments for another. When it comes to the primacy of the biblical text, many contemporary Americans are not quite one with their predecessors, who touted its merits at every turn and in every possible form, from hoax to Hollywood ballyhoo. In some quarters, our attitude toward the commandments is likely to be far less dutiful and more knowing, even ironic, much like the perspective of the celebrated contemporary comedians who have taken them down a peg or two. "Oops," said Moses in Mel Brooks's *History of the World, Part One*, as the third of three ancient tablets, bearing an additional five commandments, slipped from his grasp and crashed on the floor of the craggy mountaintop, changing history—and numerology—forever. Even ten were too many, insisted George Carlin, who deftly whittled them down to the bare minimum. "Two is all you need, folks. Moses could have carried them down the hill in his pocket."[2]

Other humorists are slightly more forgiving, but only just. In modern-day America, hardly a year goes by without a succession of *New Yorker* cartoons that pokes fun at the Ten Commandments and gently skewers America's fondness for them. I am drawn to one particularly telling cartoon, the handiwork of Robert Mankoff, in which a crowd has gathered at the foot of Mount Sinai to greet Moses, who clasps the two tablets to his chest. On the perimeter of the crowd, a man gesticulates madly in an attempt to get Moses's attention, so that he might pointedly ask him, "What's the take-away on all this?"[3]

When not tickling our funny bone, the tablets of the law have also become the stuff of controversy, a litmus test of political conviction. Politics guides our estimation of them. Our respective location on the political spectrum determines whether our stance is consensual or confrontational, welcoming or wary. Those on the Right are quick to embrace the Ten Commandments as an ongoing, and still viable, symbol of the nation's heritage and history, while those on the Left are just as quick to reject them as a pair of cultural blinders that fail to acknowledge just how much the nation has changed over time. Meanwhile, those who find themselves smack in the middle of the political spectrum, who understand both the celebrated historicity and the fraught contemporaneity of the commandments, are unsure of what to do with them. One way or another, the Ten Commandments roil and fragment the commonweal of the twenty-first century.

Back in Sid Grauman's day, though—indeed, for most of modern American history—the Ten Commandments had a different calling: they brought people together. For a country whose diverse population was often bound by little other than geography and the good fortune of calling the United States its home, the Ten Commandments were both rallying point and common ground. So highly valued, so appealing were they that different groups of Americans sought repeatedly to extend their reach. Insinuating the Ten Commandments deeper and deeper within the body politic, some insisted on their indigenousness, others promoted them as the law of the land, and still others devised entirely new forms of visual expression to capture their allure. At times, champions of the Ten Commandments went to such great lengths to strengthen their hold that they bore false witness, blasphemed, worshipped graven images, and dishonored the ways of their parents. In the name of the Ten Commandments, someone from Ohio pulled a fast one on the American public; Charles Walters, the Kansas politician, endured the taunts of his fellow legislators; and congregants at the Norfolk Street Synagogue in New York rose up against the unusually shaped window that graced their sanctuary. In the name of the Ten Commandments, Americans also instituted therapeutic regimens, spent millions of dollars on eye-popping special effects, and even transformed the lawgiver into a toy.

So, what is the takeaway on all this? Why did earlier generations of Americans make so much of them? Why did they act, now and again, as if they, rather than the ancient Israelites, had stood at Sinai? The answer is as simple and unvarnished as counting

Whatever form it assumed—print or photograph, statuary or jewelry—the Ten Commandments exerted a strong pull on the American body politic, and still does. *Library of Congress, Prints and Photographs Division, LC-DIG, ppmsca-15862*

America's practice of ranking ideas and experiences in terms of a top ten list owes its origins to the Ten Commandments. *Library of Congress, Prints and Photographs Division, LC-DIG-ds-09332*

from one to ten: the Ten Commandments furnished America with a pedigree. The Old World had its castles and coats of arms. The New World had the Ten Commandments. Plainspoken, much like the American people, the biblical covenant heightened the nation's sense of election, buttressing its claim to be a latter-day Promised Land. In the Old World, depictions of the Ten Commandments were customarily found within an ecclesiastical setting where they were seen as relics of the past—and laid low. In the New World, the Ten Commandments floated free of their traditional context and meaning, assuming a new lease on life. In the Old World, the two tablets of the law were encumbered, even shattered. In the New, they stood tall and whole: a vibrant, assertive presence. Conferring confidence and authority, the Ten Commandments safeguarded the United States. In Los Angeles and Dubuque, New York and

Topeka, their combination of discipline and agency, of responsibility and possibility, held out the promise of order and stability, of keeping the nation intact. In their formulation of the ties that bound the individual and the community, the Ten Commandments provided a structure in which freedom flourished.

You had God's word on that.

ACKNOWLEDGMENTS

During the many years it took to complete this book, I often felt one with the ancient Israelites, wandering about the desert with no resolution in sight. A cascade of events—the death of my mother, followed all too quickly by the loss of my father; the challenges of a new academic position; the sudden, and then protracted, illness of my husband—prevented me from reaching my destination—"the end"—as expeditiously as I had anticipated. Like my forebears, I too grew querulous from time to time, but my frustrations, unlike theirs, were eased considerably by the many people—archivists and curators, historians and lawyers, theologians and just plain folks—who offered a helping hand and lent a willing ear along the way.

I owe a profound debt of gratitude to the John W. Kluge Center of the Library of Congress, where, for several glorious months as a Distinguished Visiting Scholar, I availed myself of its unparalleled treasures, setting this book in motion. To Michael Grunberger, former head, Hebraic Section, of the Library of Congress, who first brought the Kluge Center to my attention and who facilitated my fellowship, go my heartiest thanks. Peggy Pearlstein, who succeeded Mr. Grunberger, was also unfailingly helpful, seeing to it that I cut as broad a swath as possible through the library's vast resources. Carolyn Brown, the former director of the Kluge Center;

Mary Lou Reker, special assistant to the director; and JoAnne Kitching, administrative specialist, created the kind of scholarly haven most of us can only dream about. I was fortunate to spend my waking hours in the company of the Library of Congress's many curators—an uncommon lot—who extended themselves mightily on my behalf. Sarah Duke, curator of popular and applied graphic art, Prints and Photographs Division, was exemplary in this regard, a researcher's best friend.

The stewards of numerous other collections and repositories fielded my inquiries and attended to my research requests with grace and efficiency. Maureen O'Connor Leach, coordinator, Trenton Historical Society, and Kathleen Maguire, the society's former head of Research Services, went beyond the call of duty, as did Kate Dietrick, assistant archivist, Upper Midwest Jewish Archives at the University of Minnesota, and Cindy Brightenburg, reference specialist at the L. Tom Perry Special Collections, Harold B. Lee Library, Brigham Young University. Patti Malenke, director of the Johnson-Humrickhouse Museum in Coshocton, Ohio, graciously responded to a barrage of questions, as did Ann K. Sindelar, reference supervisor at Cleveland's Western Reserve Historical Society. My colleague, Brad Sabin Hill, former curator of the Edward I. Kiev Collection at the George Washington University, was a steady fount of suggestions and citations. Many people throughout the country were kind enough to furnish me with all sorts of fascinating material, enriching this study. Their ranks include James D'Arc, curator, Arts and Communications Archives, L. Tom Perry Special Collections, Harold B. Lee Library, Brigham Young University; Tanya Elder, archivist at the American Jewish Historical Society, Center for Jewish History in New York; Karen Falk, curator, the Jewish Museum of Maryland; Robert Horton, chair, Archives Center, National Museum of American History, Smithsonian Institution, and his knowledgeable staff, as well as Mallory Warner of the museum's division of Medicine & Science; Andrea Immel, curator of Princeton's Cotsen Children's Library;

Judy Margles, director of the Oregon Jewish Museum and Center for Holocaust Education, and Anne Levant Prahl, its curator of collections; Randy Scott, comic art bibliographer, Special Collections Division, Michigan State Library; Wendy Turman, deputy director, the Jewish Historical Society of Greater Washington, and Kristine Krueger, coordinator of the National Film Information Service, Margaret Herrick Library of the Academy of Motion Picture Arts & Sciences.

Gary Zola, executive director of the Jacob Rader Marcus Center of the American Jewish Archives in Cincinnati, and Kevin Proffitt, its senior archivist for research and collections, provided unstinting and generous assistance throughout the life of this project. Kenneth Cobb, director of New York City's Municipal Archives, was always at the ready to assist my forays into the past. I would also like to acknowledge the late Al Orensanz, executive director of the Angel Orensanz Foundation, for allowing me the run of 172 Norfolk Street in downtown Manhattan one fine spring afternoon, and Amy Mallor, executive director of San Francisco's Congregation Sherith Israel, for permission to publish an image of its much-vaunted stained-glass window. I'm particularly grateful to Larry McCallister, vice president of licensing for Paramount Pictures, and Kay Peterson of the Rights and Reproductions Department of the National Museum of American History for making it possible to publish images from their respective collections without burning a hole in my pocket.

The opportunity to present my thoughts, and in various stages of development, was a real boon. I benefited enormously from collegial exchanges at the American Jewish Archives, Columbia University, Georgetown University, the Library of Congress, NYU, Princeton University, Stanford University, Yale University, the University of Maryland, the University of Michigan, and Vanderbilt University, as well as from numerous scholar-in-residencies at congregations throughout the country. Lay audiences listened attentively to my musings, offered all kinds of sensible suggestions in response and on several occasions even brought me things from their homes—artwork, books, jewelry—they thought I should see.

Productive conversations also took place in hotel lobbies and university hallways, over dinner, on the train, and via e-mail. For their smart insights and bright suggestions, I warmly thank Harry Baumgarten, Sara Bershtel, Marc Brettler, Jeffrey J. Cohen, Marc Dollinger, Yaacob Dweck, Rabbi Ezra Finkelstein, Alice T. Friedman, Bill Gleason, Carol Goldberg, Lisa Gordis, Adam Gregerman, Sam Gruber, Joseph Haker, Dirk Hartog, Ava Kahn, Shaul Kellner, David Koffman, Philip Jenkins, Josh Lambert, Chip Lupu, Natan Meier, Robert Orsi, Bill Plevan, Sally Promey, Christopher Rollston, Jonathan Rosen, Starry Schor, Jeffrey Shandler, Mark Slobin, Chaim Steinberger, Marc Stern, Bill Tuttle, Steve Weitzman, Leon Wieseltier, Jacob Wisse, Bob Wuthnow, and Froma Zeitlin. I'm grateful also to the anonymous reviewers of my manuscript, whose suggestions were astute and generous. Every conversation I have had with Barbara Kirshenblatt-Gimblett about the Ten Commandments—or anything else, for that matter—was a clarifying and inspiring one. Klara Palotai's enthusiasm for and prowess at historical sleuthing, at untangling the mystery of the Ten Commandments stained-glass window at the former Congregation Anshi Chesed, deserves special mention. I am indebted to my students at the George Washington University and Princeton University who, over the years, took my seminar on the role of the Ten Commandments in American culture, enlivening the proceedings with their good ideas and good cheer.

When it came to cheering me on, my dedicated agent and stalwart pal Josh Getzler and his associate, Danielle Burby, of the HSG Agency did yeoman's service. At Oxford University Press, Nancy Toff's keen eye and even keener ear for the felicities—and infelicities—of language kept me on track throughout, as did Elda Granata's careful attention to detail. Danielle Michaely's sensitive copyediting and Julia Turner's patience and skill smoothly translated a manuscript into a book.

The generosity of George Washington University's History Department, ably presided over by Katrin Schultheiss, and that of the Dean's Office of George Washington University's Columbian College of Arts & Sciences enabled the book to shine visually.

My beloved Joz enabled me to shine. In celebration of his keen intelligence, high moral sensitivity, and largeness of spirit, I dedicate this book to him.

NOTES

Introduction

1. "The Inquiring Reporter: The Question," *Chicago Daily Tribune*, August 12, 1921, 13.

2. "Says Few Churchmen Know the Decalogue," *New York Times*, March 9, 1927, 20.

3. "Be Above It, Never Covet," *God's Top 10*, Brentwood Music (Brentwood, TN, 1996). Words and Music by Troy Nilsson and Genie Nilsson. The song is to be sung "brightly." Leonard Felson, "Throwing Out the Ten Commandments—The Ones That Sat Atop My Cake," *Tablet*, December 19, 2013. George Dugan, "American Jewish Committee Salutes Five Cardinals," *New York Times*, November 14, 1966, 37.

4. http://www.orientaltrading.com/ten-commandments-cardboard-stand-up-a2-36.

5. For Africans, explains Philip Jenkins, an astute observer of the latest trends in Christianity, the "verse means what it says, avoiding other gods." See Jenkins, *The New Faces of Christianity: Believing the Bible in the Global South* (New York: Oxford University Press, 2006), 51; personal communication with Philip Jenkins, January 19, 2016.

6. Martin Luther King Jr., *Why We Can't Wait* (New York: Harper & Row, 1964), chap. 4. The pledge is also widely available online. Several years later, at a 1968 antiwar demonstration in New York's Central Park, Coretta Scott King read aloud from what she called the "Ten Commandments on Vietnam." To mounting applause, she told the protesters that she had found "some notes taken from [her] husband's pockets upon his death" that

suggested that Dr. King might have prepared "his Vietnam Decalogue" for the rally. "The decalogue," King's widow added, "had never been made public before." "Mrs. King Reads War Decalogue," *New York Times,* April 28, 1968, 73.

7. George E. Sokolsky, "These Days: In God We Trust," *Washington Post,* July 2, 1962, A19; "A Holiday Proposed for the Decalogue," *New York Times,* June 19, 1963, 34. It took a while—nearly fifty years—before that proposal was actually implemented. In 2006, the Ten Commandments Commission, a largely Christian public interest group dismayed by the recent Supreme Court rulings about the display of the Ten Commandments, designated the first Sunday in May as "Ten Commandments Day." An act of restoration as well as an exercise in defiance, the holiday appealed to "those who care about traditional values [and who] cannot passively sit by and watch the removal of one of the very principles that made this country great." The Ten Commandments Commission maintains an active web presence at http://www.tencommandmentsday.com/. On Morgan, see "Must Know the Commandments," *Chicago Daily Tribune,* January 2, 1897, 13. Although his proposition did not secure enough votes to pass, it did enjoy the support of nearly twenty percent of the country's senators. On colonial America's affinity for the Bible and its reliance on scriptural authority, see Mark A. Noll, *In the Beginning Was the Word: The Bible in American Public Life, 1492-1783* (New York: Oxford University Press, 2015).

8. "A Plea for the Ten Commandments," *Reformed Church Messenger,* February 24, 1869, 6.

9. "Laugh at the Ten Commandments, all you want, Dan, but they pack an awful wallop," reads one of the intertitles in Cecil B. DeMille's 1923 film, *The Ten Commandments.*

Chapter 1

1. W. D. Beekham, correspondent for the *Cincinnati Commercial,* cited by D. Francis Bacon, "The Ohio 'Holy Stone,'" *Harper's Weekly* 4, no. 192 (September 1860): 545; Isaac Smucker, "Who Were the Aboriginals of North America?," *The Ladies Repository,* April 1, 1862, 243; "Remarkable Archaeological Discovery in Ohio—Letter to the Editor from D.," *New York Times,* July 27, 1860, 2; Colonel Charles Whittlesey, "Archaeological Frauds—Inscriptions Attributed to the Mound Builders—Three Remarkable Forgeries," Western Reserve Historical Society. *Historical and Archaeological Tracts, Number 9,* Cleveland, Ohio, February 1872, 3.

2. "The Two Hebrew Inscriptions Found in Ohio," *The Independent*, March 14, 1861, 2; W. D. Beekham cited in D. Francis Bacon, "The Ohio 'Holy Stone,'" 545. No one suspected Mr. Wyrick or his champions of "being parties to another Mormon imposture." See, for example, "The Ohio Relic," *The Independent*, March 14, 1861, 4; Whittlesey, "Archaeological Frauds," 3; Charles Whittlesey, "Fugitive Essays upon Interesting and Useful Subjects, Relating to the Early History of Ohio, Its Geology and Architecture. A Dissertation upon the Antiquity of the Material Universe" (Hudson, OH: Sawyer, Ingersoll and Co., 1852); Whittlesey, "Archaeological Frauds," p. 4.

3. D. Francis Bacon, "The Ohio 'Holy Stone,'" 546; Bacon, "The Ohio 'Holy Stone,'" p. 545; "The 'Hebrew Stone' in Ohio," Letter to the Editor from Mr. Henry R. Schoolcraft, *New York Times*, August 6, 1860, 3. Additional details about Mr. Wyrick and his discoveries can be found in Robert W. Alrutz's indispensable account, "The Newark Holy Stones: The History of an Archaeological Tragedy," *Journal of Scientific Laboratories [Denison University]*, 1980, 1–72.

4. "The Hebrew-Inscribed Stones Found in Ohio: The Description Deciphered," *New York Evangelist*, April 4, 1861, 3; John Winspeace McCarty, "Another Holy Stone: Where It Was Found," *The Israelite*, November 9, 1860, 146; Reverend A. Fischel, "The Hebrew-Inscribed Stones Found in Ohio," *Jewish Messenger*, June 21, 1861, 189; Gerald Fowke, *Archaeological History of Ohio: The Mound Builders and Later Indians* (Columbus, OH: Ohio State Archaeological and Historical Society, 1902), 581; "The Hebrew-Inscribed Stones Found in Ohio," *New York Evangelist*, April 4, 1861, 3.

5. Alan Taylor, "The Early Republic's Supernatural Economy: Treasure Seeking in the American Northeast, 1780-1830," *American Quarterly* 38 (1986): 6–34; David Wyrick, "Further about the Holy Stone," *The Israelite*, November 16, 1860, 157; McCarty, "Another Holy Stone," 146; "The Ohio Mounds—Stupendous Monuments of a Departed Race," *Cincinnati Daily Enquirer*, November 26, 1866; Reverend M. R. Miller, "Sacred Stones of the Vicinity of Newark, Licking County, Ohio," *Occident and American Jewish Advocate* XXIV, no. 3 (June 1866): 109; Reverend M. R. Miller, "Sacred Stones of the Vicinity of Newark, Licking County, Ohio," *Occident and American Jewish Advocate* XXIV, no. 2 (May 1866): 75.

6. Miller, "Sacred Stones," *Occident and American Jewish Advocate* XXIV, no. 2 (May 1866): 75; Miller, "Sacred Stones," *Occident and American Jewish Advocate* XXIV, no. 3 (June 1866): 108; Joseph S. Unzicker Scrapbook,

1849–1869, MS 4373, Western Reserve Historical Society, Cleveland, Ohio; personal exchange with Ann K. Sindelar, reference supervisor, Library Research Center, Western Reserve Historical Society, December 20, 2014, and February 2, 2015.

7. Mayer Sulzberger, "The Alphabet of the Decalogue-Stone Found Near Newark, Ohio," *Occident and American Jewish Advocate* XXV, no. 10 (January 1868): 526; Bernard Felsenthal to David Johnson, November 19, 1866, 1, Johnson-Humrickhouse Museum Archives. I would like to thank Patti Malenke, director of the Johnson-Humrickhouse Museum, for bringing this document to my attention. The learned men of the American Ethnological Society were not the only ones to have handled these artifacts. According to Rabbi David Philipson, two of Cincinnati's prominent rabbis at the time, Max Lilienthal and Bernard Illowy, also examined them. See David Philipson, "Are There Traces of the Ten Lost Tribes in Ohio?," *Publications of the American Jewish Historical Society* no. 13 (1905): 43; Smucker, "Who Were the Aboriginals?," 244; Miller, "Sacred Stones," *Occident and American Jewish Advocate* XXIV, no. 2 (May 1866): 73; "The Hebrew-Inscribed Stones Found in Ohio," *New York Evangelist,* April 4, 1861, 3; Miller, "Sacred Stones," *Occident and American Jewish Advocate* XXIV, no. 2 (May 1866): 75.

8. "The Bureau of Ethnology's Efforts to Ascertain Who They Were. From The Washington Star," *New York Times,* September 27, 1895, 5; Smucker, "Who Were the Aboriginals?," 239; "The Mound Builders," *New York Times,* October 31, 1875, 9. See also Robert Silverberg, *Mound Builders of Ancient America: The Archaeology of a Myth* (Greenwich, CT: New York Graphic Society, 1968); Henry R. Schoolcraft cited in Annette Kolodny, "Fictions from American Prehistory: Indians, Archaeology and National Origins Myths," *American Literature* 75, no. 4 (December 2003): 696; Smucker, "Who Were the Aboriginals?," 242.

9. "Bureau of Ethnology's Efforts," *New York Times,* September 27, 1895, 5. The proof text to which Isaac Smucker referred read as follows: "As Moses the servant of the Lord commanded the children of Israel, as it is written in the book of the law of Moses, an altar of unhewn stones, upon which no man has lifted up any iron; and they offered thereon burnt-offerings unto the Lord, and sacrificed peace-offerings. And he wrote there upon the stones a copy of the law of Moses, which he wrote before the children of Israel." Smucker, "Who Were the Aboriginals?," 243; Fischel, "The Hebrew-Inscribed Stones," *Jewish Messenger,* 189.

10. "Our Early Jews," *New York Times,* January 27, 1880, 4.

11. "The Ohio Holy Stone," *The Independent*, February 14, 1861, 2; Bradley T. Lepper and Jeff Gill report that Smucker subsequently changed his mind and disavowed the authenticity of Wyrick's finds. See Bradley T. Lepper and Jeff Gill, "The Newark Holy Stones," *Timeline* 17, no. 3 (May–June 2000): 20; Philipson quoting Dr. Abraham Geiger, "Are There Traces?," 44; Whittlesey, "Archaeological Frauds," 1; "Remarkable Archaeological Discovery in Ohio—Letter to the Editor from D.," *New York Times*, July 27, 1860, 2; Whittlesey, "Archaeological Frauds," 4.

12. McCarty, "Another Holy Stone," 146; David Wyrick to John Henry, April 13, 1863, cited in J. Huston McCulloch, "The Newark Hebrew Stones: Wyrick's Letter to Joseph Henry," *Midwest Epigraphic Journal* 6 (1989): 5–10; Nathan Brown to David M. Johnson, December 16, 1871, Johnson-Humrickhouse Museum Archives; David Wyrick, *A representation of the two stones with the characters inscribed upon them that were found by D. Wyrick during the summer of 1860. Near Newark, Ohio. 1860*, 13.

13. Wyrick, *Representation*, 8, 9, 13.

14. Whittlesey, "Archaeological Frauds," 3; Bacon, "The Ohio 'Holy Stone,'" 546; Whittlesey, "Archaeological Frauds," 4; Philipson, "Are There Traces?," 44.

15. "The Ohio Mounds—Stupendous Monuments of a Departed Race," *Cincinnati Daily Enquirer*, November 26, 1866.

16. Philipson, "Are There Traces?," 43; Bernard Felsenthal to David Johnson, November 19, 1866, 2, Johnson-Humrickhouse Museum Archives; Advertisement in *The Occident and American Jewish Advocate* XXV, no. 11 (February 1868): 594.

17. Nathan Brown to David Johnson, December 16, 1871, Johnson-Humrickhouse Museum Archives; Ben Hoover, "Coshocton's Museum Has Holy Stones," *Newark Advocate and American Tribune*, October 22, 1934, 2, 4, and 11.

18. See the webpage of the Johnson-Humrickhouse Museum, especially "Gift Shop: Newark Holy Stone Materials" (http://www.jhmuseum.org); personal exchange with Patti Malenke about the identity of Wyrick's current champions, January 14–15, 2015; webpage of the Johnson-Humrickhouse Museum, "On View: Newark Holy Stones"; Jeffrey Jerome Cohen, "Stories of Stone," *postmedieval: a journal of medieval cultural studies* 1 (2010): 60.

19. Silverberg, *Mound Builders*, 209, 211. Some of the most current theories include the following: Bradley T. Lepper and Jeff Gill, "The Newark Holy

Stones," *Timeline* 17, no. 3 (May–June 2000): 17–25; Dr. Yitzchok Levine, "Aseres Hashevatim: In America?," *Mishpacha*, Ellul 5770, 13–15; David A. Deal, "The Ohio Decalog: A Case of Fraudulent Archaeology," *Ancient American* 2, no. 11 (January–February 1996): 10–19.

20. Rochelle I. Altman, "'First . . . Recognize That It's a Penny': Report on the 'Newark' Ritual Artifacts," http://www.bibleinterp.com/articles/Altman_ Newark.shtml; Fischel, "The Hebrew-Inscribed Stones," 189. "I consider it not impossible," Fischel wrote in 1861, "that this particular mound may have been re-opened within the last 370 years, and that the Indians deposited in the tombs these stones, which they had stolen from some of the European settlers."

21. Isaac Mayer Wise, *Moses: The Man and Statesman* (Cincinnati: Bloch & Company, 1883), 27.

22. On the fertile soil of Ohio, see, for example, "Remarkable Archaeological Discovery in Ohio—Letter to the Editor from D.," *New York Times*, July 27, 1860, 2; *The Autobiography of Cecil B. DeMille*, ed. Donald Hayne (Englewood Cliffs, NJ: Prentice-Hall, 1959), 253; "Many Lands: Within the Boundaries of Southern California Are Photographed Scenes from Every Country on the Face of the Globe. Here the Motion Picture Scenes of Foreign Countries Are Found," *Los Angeles Times*, January 2, 1929, D14. See also "DeMille Is to Begin on Bible Play," *Los Angeles Times*, April 24, 1923, I10.

23. For details, as well as vivid pictures, of the set, see "The Lost City of DeMille," *Grand Street* 13, no. 1 (1994): 198–207; "Plan Massive Production," *Los Angeles Times*, April 12, 1923, I16; Robert S. Birchard, *Cecil B. DeMille's Hollywood* (Lexington: University of Kentucky Press, 2004), 183; "What Becomes of Big Sets," *Los Angeles Times*, May 11, 1924, X5; Henry MacMahon, "The Decline and Fall of a Plaster Empire," *New-York Tribune*, December 16, 1923, SM11. A local church made use of the timber, while several of the sphinxes made their way to the entrance of the city of Santa Maria, California.

24. Peter Brosnan cited in Joe Payne, "Epic Excavation," *Santa Maria Sun*, June 4, 2013, http://www.santamariasun.com/cover/9843/epic-excavation/; "The Fight to Preserve DeMille's Lost City," Weekend Edition, NPR, February 12, 2005; "Movie History Stored," *Los Angeles Times*, August 11, 1929, B13; Peter Fish, "Raiders of the Lost City," *Sunset*, October 1997, 15. For additional information about the dig, see Dennis Drabelle, "Ancient Egypt on the Pacific," *Preservation*, July/August 1996, 40–44; "Sphinx Unearthed from 1923 Cecil B. DeMille Movie Set," *Los*

Angeles Times, October 17, 2014; Laura Geggel, "Giant Sphinx from Ten Commandments Film Unearthed 91 Years Later," *Live Science,* October 27, 2014, http://www.livescience.com/48321-ten-commandments-sphinx-unearthed.html; "Under the Dunes, a City by DeMille," *New York Times,* November 6, 1990, A11.

25. See the website of the Guadalupe-Nipomo Dunes Center, especially "The Lost City of DeMille"; Mike Anton, "Digging Up a Piece of Hollywood History," *Los Angeles Times,* March 18, 2010.

26. I would like to acknowledge the contribution of Mary Oakley Strasser, who, in connection with a seminar I taught in 2009 at Princeton University on the Ten Commandments in American culture, shared with me the photographs she had taken in March of that year of the "Lost City of DeMille" exhibition. Peter Brosnan was quoted in Anton, "Digging Up a Piece of Hollywood History."

27. "The Ten Commandments Granite Monolith," one-page document sent by the Fraternal Order of Eagles to its members, n.d., Cecil B. DeMille Papers, Mss. 1400, Box 990, Folder 6, L. Tom Perry Special Collections, Harold B. Lee Library, Brigham Young University.

28. In early July 2015, as I wrote these words, the Oklahoma Supreme Court ruled that a Ten Commandments monument on the grounds of the Oklahoma capitol, which had been erected in 2012, had to be removed. "It violates the state's constitutional ban on using public property to benefit a religion," the court explained, noting that the Ten Commandments were "obviously religious in nature and are an integral part of the Jewish and Christian faiths." See, for example, "Commandments Monument Cannot Remain, Court Rules," *New York Times,* July 1, 2015, A17, and Heide Brandes, "Oklahoma's Top Court Says State Must Remove Ten Commandments Monument," July 21, 2015, http://www.huffingtonpost.com/entry/oklahoma-ten-commandments.

29. Jess Bravin, "When Moses' Law Runs Afoul of the US's, Get Me Cecil B. DeMille," *Wall Street Journal,* April 18, 2001, A1; Francis Schroeder, "Thou Shalt Not," *Eagle* 41, no. 3 (March 1953): 14–15. On Judge Ruegemer's campaign, see, for example, "Youth Guidance Aims Gain Impetus from Ten Commandments Plan," *Eagle* 42, no. 9 (October 1954): 26; personal exchange with Joseph Haker, June 4 and 11, 2013, whose forthcoming thesis from the University of Minnesota explores the postwar history of the Eagles. Hoover's endorsement can be found on the back of any copy of the Ten Commandments paper scroll produced by the Eagles. The one I consulted

was housed in the American Jewish Congress Papers, Record Group I-77, Box 334, Folder 3, American Jewish Historical Society, Center for Jewish History, New York.

30. "Eagles in Brave Parade," *New York Times*, September 3, 1903, 5; "Eagles in Fine Feathers," *New York Times*, August 30, 1903, 12; "Set in Stone by DeMille," *Variety*, March 7–13, 2005, 4, clipping found in folder marked "Ten Commandments, 1956," Special Collections, New York Public Library for the Performing Arts; "Wagner Praises Order of Eagles," *New York Times*, July 26, 1957, 17; Fraternal Order of Eagles, *On Eagle Wings*, 1957–58, next-to-last page, Comic Art Collection, Michigan State University Libraries.

31. "Inter-Office Communication from Ann del Valle to Mr. DeMille," May 23, 1956, 2, Cecil B. DeMille Papers, Mss. 1400, Box 490, Folder 1.

32. *On Eagle Wings*, next-to-last page; Art Arthur to Judge E. J. Ruegemer, July 14, 1955, Cecil B. DeMille Papers, Mss. 1400, Box 990, Folder 6.

33. Yul Brynner, "Ten Commandments Monolith Unveiled," *Eagle* 45, no. 4 (April 1957): 20.

34. "Ten Commandments in Stone Unveiled by Local Eagles," *Trenton Sunday Times-Advertiser*, November 4, 1956, Part One, n.p.

35. "Truth," *Eagle* 42, no. 2 (February 1954): 42.

36. Memorandum from Samuel Lewis Gaber to Leo Pfeffer, March 28, 1958, American Jewish Congress Papers, Box 334, Folder 3; "Art Board Rejects Tablet with Ten Commandments," clipping from the *Philadelphia Evening Bulletin*, March 22, 1958, American Jewish Congress Papers, Box 334, Folder 3; clipping from *Philadelphia Inquirer*, December 22, 1958, American Jewish Congress Papers, Box 334, folder marked "CLSA Subject File: Religious Symbols on Public Property, Ten Commandments Correspondence, Reports and Court Documents, 1956-57"; "Religious Symbols on Public Property," *American Jewish Year Book* 61 (1960): 38.

37. Telegram sent by Rabbi Julius Nodel to Albert Vorspan, December 10, 1958, American Jewish Congress Papers, Box 334, Folder 3.

38. Over the years, and as recently as February 2015, Marc Stern, currently the associate general counsel of the American Jewish Committee, was of invaluable assistance when it came both to understanding the history of church-state relations in postwar America and to contextualizing the work of the American Jewish Congress, with which he was long and intimately familiar. Time and again, whether over lunch or in the classroom, Mr. Stern was the most generous of colleagues. For additional background

information, see Leo Pfeffer, *Church, State, and Freedom* (Boston: Beacon Press, 1953), and Anson Phelps Stokes, "Among Our Basic Liberties," *New York Times*, September 13, 1953, BR37. The voluminous papers of the American Jewish Congress, Record Group I-77, are a part of the holdings of the American Jewish Historical Society, Center for Jewish History, New York City. For the purposes of this study, Boxes 327, 333, and 334 were the most germane. On the American Jewish Congress's growing awareness of the scope of the Eagles campaign, see, especially, Memorandum from Jules Cohen to the Joint Advisory Committee, March 24, 1958, American Jewish Congress Papers, Box 334, Folder 3; "Memorandum of Law in Opposition to Display of the Ten Commandments on Public School Premises," May 1957, 3; American Jewish Congress Papers, Box 334, Folder 1 (hereafter "Memorandum").

39. Letter from Leo Pfeffer to Rabbi Albert Minda, July 2, 1957, American Jewish Congress Papers, Box 333, folder marked "CLSA Subject Files: Religious Symbols on Public Property, Ten Commandments Correspondence, Mimeographs and Releases, 1956-57"; Edwin A. Bennett to the Honorable Frank Kryzan, June 21, 1957, American Jewish Congress Papers, Box 333, folder marked "CLSA Subject Files: Religious Symbols on Public Property, Ten Commandments Correspondence, Mimeographs and Releases, 1956-57"; Joseph Minsky to Leo Pfeffer, April 25, 1957, American Jewish Congress Papers, Box 333, folder marked "CLSA Subject Files: Religious Symbols on Public Property, Ten Commandments Correspondence, Mimeographs and Releases, 1956-57"; Bennett to Kryzan, June 21, 1957.

40. "Memorandum," 9. See also Samuel Scheiner to Judge E. J. Ruegemer, March 27, 1958, American Jewish Congress Papers, Box 334, Folder 3.

41. "Memorandum," 4.

42. "Memorandum," 20, 21, 19, 22.

43. Albert Vorspan to Rabbi Norman Diamond, January 27, 1959, American Jewish Congress Papers, Box 334, Folder 3; Joseph Minsky to Leo Pfeffer, May 14, 1957, American Jewish Congress Papers, Box 333, folder marked "CLSA Subject Files: Religious Symbols on Public Property, Ten Commandments Correspondence, Mimeographs and Releases, 1956-57"; Leo Pfeffer to Rabbi Minda, July 2, 1957, and July 10, 1957, American Jewish Congress Papers, Box 333, folder marked "CLSA Subject Files: Religious Symbols on Public Property, Ten Commandments Correspondence, Mimeographs and Releases, 1956-57."

44. Donald Hayne to Cecil B. DeMille, August 27, 1957, Cecil B. DeMille Collection, Mss. 1400, Box 490, Folder 1. Years before, when first embarking on his campaign to post paper versions of the Ten Commandments, Judge Ruegemer had reached out to Rabbi Minda, seeking—and receiving—his endorsement. When, in July 1957, it came belatedly to the rabbi's attention that the modest paper version he had once championed had now developed into an overgrown stone pillar to be housed on public property, the clergyman had a change of heart. "Whatever may have been in my mind at that time," Minda told Ruegemer, "I am now convinced, particularly in light of recent trends that the efforts to place these plaques [*sic*] in institutions and places, state-sponsored, represents a serious threat to and departure from the classic American principle of separation of Church-State." Accordingly, I must ask that "my name not be used in any efforts to have [the Ten Commandments] placed in any institution or sites, state sponsored or owned. I trust you will understand my position." See Draft of Letter from Rabbi Albert Minda to Judge E. J. Ruegemer, July 10, 1957, and Leo Pfeffer to Rabbi Albert Minda, July 17, 1957, American Jewish Congress Papers, Box 333, folder marked "CLSA Subject Files: Religious Symbols on Public Property, Ten Commandments Correspondence, Mimeographs and Releases, 1956-57," as well as E. J. Ruegemer to Donald Hayne, August 23, 1957, Cecil B. DeMille Papers, Mss. 1400, Box 490, Folder 1. Rabbi Minda's position on the Ten Commandments was nothing if not consistent with his views on church–state relations more generally. In his capacity as chairman of the Committee on Church and State of the Central Conference of American Rabbis, Albert Minda had long been a champion of the First Amendment. Religion, he argued in a presentation before the National Community Relations Advisory Council in 1944, is an "imperative necessity," but not one in which the state should be involved. See, for example, "Religious Education and Public Schools," November 14, 1944, Albert Minda Papers, folder marked "Sermons, Church and State, Economy, Daily Living, 1957," Minnesota Historical Society.

45. Mordaunt Hall, "King of Kings: Cecil B. DeMille's Picture of the Life of Christ Is an Impressive Piece of Work," *New York Times*, April 24, 1957, X5; "Dr. Wise Denounces the 'King of Kings,'" *New York Times*, December 5, 1927, 30. See also "Protest 'King of Kings:' Jewish Ministers Oppose Showing Film as Cause of Prejudice," *New York Times*, December 31, 1927, 12; "King of Kings Film Will Be Revised: DeMille to Change Scenes and Titles as Jews Asked and Add a Foreword," *New York Times*, January 6, 1928, 16. For more on the Jewish response to the film, see Felicia Herman, "The

Most Dangerous Anti-Semitic Photoplay in Filmdom: American Jews and the 'King of Kings,' " *Velvet Light Trap* 46 (Fall 2000): 12–25; Yael Ohad-Karny, "Anticipating Gibson's 'The Passion of the Christ': The Controversy over Cecil B. DeMille's 'The King of Kings,' " *Jewish History* 19, no. 2 (2005): 189–210.

46. Donald Hayne to the Honorable E. J. Ruegemer, September 12, 1957, 1, Cecil B. DeMille Papers, Mss. 1400, Box 490, Folder 1; Donald Hayne to Cecil B. DeMille, August 27, 1957, Cecil B. DeMille Papers, Mss. 1400, Box 490, Folder 1. Donald Hayne to the Honorable E. J. Ruegemer, September 12, 1957, especially p. 2, contains a host of recommendations on how to subdue the opposition.

47. "The Editor's Mail: H.E. Simon, 'Ten Commandments,' " *Eagle* 45, no. 4 (April 1957): 6. The Eagles' official response followed immediately thereafter.

48. Memorandum from Benjamin W. Mintz to Leo Pfeffer, July 29, 1957, American Jewish Congress Papers, Box 333, folder marked "CLSA Subject Files: Religious Symbols on Public Property, Ten Commandments Correspondence, Mimeographs and Releases, 1956-57." On the Eagles' enthusiastic embrace of this project, see, for example, Manny Meyers, "An Eagle Project Makes New Friends: Spreading the Commandments," *Eagle* 42, no. 7 (July 1954): 18–19; "How the Scrolls Are Prepared," *Eagle* 42, no. 7 (July 1954): 18–19; and Sue Hoffman, "The Real History of the Ten Commandments Project of the Fraternal Order of Eagles," http://www.religioustolerance,org/hoffman01.htm.

49. "Newark Agog over Biblical Plaque in High School," unidentified clipping, ca. 1956, American Jewish Congress Papers, Box 333, folder marked "CLSA Subject Files: Religious Symbols on Public Property, Ten Commandments Correspondence, Mimeographs and Releases, 1956-57"; "Legion to Bid Schools Post Commandments," *Newsday*, January 3, 1957, clipping in American Jewish Congress Papers, Box 334, Folder 2; "Religion Plan Fought," *New York Times*, February 19, 1958, 30; "Memorandum," 2, 4, 9. On the American Jewish Congress's position on the Ten Commandments in public schools, see "American Jewish Congress Opposes New York State Bill to Introduce Revised Ten Commandments in Public Schools," American Jewish Congress Press Release, February 19, 1958, American Jewish Congress Papers, Box 334, folder marked "CLSA Subject Files: Religious Symbols on Public Property, Ten Commandments Correspondence, Mimeographs and Releases, 1958-1973"; Memorandum

from Leo Pfeffer to Phil Baum, February 14, 1958; Memorandum from Leo Pfeffer to Shad Polier, July 2, 1958, and Phil Baum to Assemblyman William Brennan, February 20, 1958, American Jewish Congress Papers, folder marked "CLSA Subject Files: Religious Symbols on Public Property, Ten Commandments Correspondence, Mimeographs and Releases, 1958-1973." Details of the American Jewish Congress's opposition to the plans of the Savannah, Georgia, school board can be found in "Report on Proposal by Grand Jury of Chatham Country to Display the Ten Commandments in the Public Schools," September 22, 1959, American Jewish Congress Papers, Box 334, folder marked "CLSA Subject Files: Religious Symbols on Public Property, Ten Commandments Correspondence, Mimeographs and Releases, 1958-1973," and Memorandum from Isaac Toubin to Leo Pfeffer, October 19, 1959, American Jewish Congress Papers, Box 334, Folder 3.

50. Joseph Minsky to Leo Pfeffer, May 14, 1957, American Jewish Congress Papers, Box 333, folder marked "CLSA Subject Files: Religious Symbols on Public Property, Ten Commandments Correspondence, Mimeographs and Releases, 1956-57." See also Dan Asher to Rabbi Norman Diamond, February 11, 1959, American Jewish Congress Papers, Box 334, Folder 3.

51. Louis Finkelstein quoted in Fred Beuttler, "For the World at Large: Intergroup Activities at the Jewish Theological Seminary," in *Tradition Renewed: A History of the Jewish Theological Seminary of America*, vol. 2, ed. Jack Wertheimer (New York: Jewish Theological Seminary of America, 1997), 698, 697. Jessica Feingold, "Up from Isolation—Intergroup Activities at the Seminary," *Judaism* 27, no. 3 (Summer 1978): 284.

52. Martin E. Marty, "Interfaith at Fifty—It Has Worked!," *Judaism* 27, no. 3 (Summer 1978): 341; Mark Silk, "Notes on the Judeo-Christian Tradition in America," *American Quarterly* 36, no. 1 (Spring 1984): 65; Marty, "Interfaith at Fifty," 341. For expressions of concern within the American Jewish community about the validity of the Judeo-Christian tradition, see, for example, Bernard Heller, "About the Judeo-Christian Tradition," *Judaism* 1, no. 3 (July 1952): 257–61, and Bernard Heller, "The Judeo-Christian Tradition Concept: Aid or Deterrent to Goodwill?," *Judaism* 2, no. 2 (April 1953): 133–39.

53. "Eagles Give Truman Print of Ten Commandments," *New York Herald Tribune*, August 19, 1952, 4; "Gift for President," *New York World Telegram and Sun*, August 20, 1952, New York World Telegram and Sun Photograph Collection, Library of Congress, Prints & Photographs; "Youth Guidance,"

Eagle 42, no. 3 (1952): 24, features a photograph of President Truman smiling as he holds aloft a framed scroll of the Ten Commandments.

54. On Van Orden, see, for example, Sylvia Moreno, "Supreme Court on a Shoestring: Homeless Man Takes on Texas Religious Display," *Washington Post*, February 21, 2005, A01; J. Souter, dissenting, *Van Orden v. Perry*, 7; Jan Jarboe Russell, "Take Two Tablets," *Texas Monthly*, February 2004, 3, 2, http://www.texasmonthly.com/politics/take-two-tablets.

55. Linda Greenhouse, "The Ten Commandments Reach the Supreme Court," *New York Times*, February 28, 2005, A12. See also Linda Greenhouse, "Justices Consider Religious Displays," *New York Times*, March 3, 2005, A18, and "The Commandments and the Court: Letters to the Editor," *New York Times*, March 4, 2005, A20.

56. "America: It's Not Just for Christians Any More (and Never Really Was)," *Church and State* 58, no. 4 (April 2005): 14.

57. J. Scalia, dissenting, *McCreary County v. American Civil Liberties Union of Kentucky*, 1–30, especially p. 24; J. Stevens, dissenting, *Van Orden v. Perry*, 27; J. O'Connor, concurring, *McCreary County v. American Civil Liberties Union of Kentucky*, 3, and Linda Greenhouse, "Justices Allow a Commandments Display, Bar Others: Context Is Cited in the Divided Decisions," *New York Times*, June 28, 2005, 1.

58. Greenhouse, "Justices Allow One Ten Commandments Display, but Bar Others," *New York Times*, June 28, 2005, A17; Opinion of C. J. Rehnquist, *Van Orden v. Perry*, 3 and 3ff; Syllabus. *Van Orden v. Perry*. No. 03-1500. Argued March 2, 2005—Decided June 27, 2005, 545 US_2005, 2; J. Breyer, concurring in judgment, *Van Orden v. Perry*, 7. On the importance of context in deciding these two cases, see Tony Mauro, "Context Is Key to Sorting Out Commandments Rulings," *First Amendment Topics*, June 28, 2005;"Justices Allow a Commandments Display, Bar Others: Context Is Cited in the Divided Decisions," *New York Times*, June 28, 2005, 1.

59. "Opinion of the Court," 15, 21; J. Breyer, concurring in judgment, *Van Orden v. Perry*, 7.

60. "Supreme Ending," *Wall Street Journal*, June 28, 2005, A14; Ralph Blumenthal, "Split Rulings on Displays Draw Praise and Dismay," *New York Times*, June 28, 2005, A17; Josh Gerstein, "High Court Verdicts Mixed on 10 Commandments," *New York Sun*, June 28, 2005, 5. See also "At the End of a Session: The Court Affirms Separation of Church and State," *New York Times*, June 28, 2005, A22. Law review articles include Vincent Phillip

Munoz, "Thou Shalt Not Post the Ten Commandments?," *Texas Review of Law and Politics* 10, no. 2 (Spring 2006): 357–400, and Ethel Brown Clement, "Public Displays of Affection . . . For God: Religious Monuments after *McCreary* and *Van Orden*," *Harvard Journal of Law and Public Policy* 31, no. 1 (Winter 2009), 231–60; Noah Feldman quoted in Josh Gerstein, "High Court Verdicts Mixed on 10 Commandments," *New York Sun,* June 28, 2005, 5.

61. Ralph Blumenthal, "Split Rulings on Displays Draw Praise and Dismay." On Moore, see Eric Velasco, "The Gospel According to Roy," *Politico Magazine,* February 11, 2015, http://www.politico.com/magazine/story/2015/02/roy-moore-alabama-gay; Richard Fausset, "For Alabama Chief Justice Soldiering in the Name of God Is Nothing New," *New York Times,* February 10, 2015, A12. Paul Finkelman, "The Ten Commandments on the Courthouse Lawn and Elsewhere," *Fordham Law Review* 73, no. 4 (March 2005): 1477–1520, esp. 1500; Joshua Green, "Roy and His Rock," *The Atlantic,* October 2005, 70–82; "Alabama Justice's Ouster Upheld in Ten Commandments Case," *New York Times,* May 1, 2004, A9.

62. "Alabama: Ten Commandments Hitting Road," *New York Times,* July 17, 2004, A10; "An Act of Faith," *Nightline,* December 8, 2004.

Chapter 2

1. "To Supplement Decalogue," *New-York Daily Tribune,* March 6, 1897, 6; Charles Parkhurst, *Our Fight with Tammany* (New York: Charles Scribner's Sons, 1895), 272. See also "The Decalogue in Kansas," *New York Times,* March 4, 1897, 6.

2. "Walters Is Irreverent," *Topeka Daily Capital,* March 3, 1897, 5.

3. The impact of the Ten Commandments on American law, legal historian Steven Green points out, was merely "illustrative or oratorical," and explicit "judicial reliance on the Ten Commandments as a source of law was all but nonexistent." Steven M. Green, "The Fount of Everything Just and Right? The Ten Commandments as a Source of American Law," *Journal of Law and Religion* 14, no. 2 (1999–2000): 554, 558.

4. "The Decalogue Bill," *Topeka State Journal,* March 8, 1897, 6; *New-York Daily Tribune,* March 21, 1897, 6; *New-York Daily Tribune,* December 21, 1898, 6. See also "Some Fool Bills," *Albany Law Journal,* April 17, 1897, 252; "To Supplement the Decalogue," *New-York Daily Tribune,* March 6, 1897, 6; *The Independent,* March 11, 1897, 49.

5. "Says 'Don't' to Cecil," *Los Angeles Times,* November 28, 1922, II6; "Modern Decalogue Favored by Pastor," *New York Times,* October 22, 1923, 19; Felix Adler, "Hollow at the Core," *New York Times,* April 22, 1895, 9.

6. Adler, "Hollow at the Core." Adler would later have a change of heart. In a 1926 speech on the occasion of the fiftieth-anniversary celebration of the Ethical Culture movement, its founder pronounced the Ten Commandments "too old-fashioned." While some of its tenets remained relevant, others, such as its prohibition against graven images, were "not what the younger generation particularly need in the way of life guidance." "Calls Decalogue Too Old-Fashioned," *New York Times,* May 13, 1926, 14.

7. "Calls Decalogue Futile," *New York Times,* May 18, 1908, 7; "Good-bye to the Decalogue," *New York Times,* May 18, 1908, 6.

8. P. W. Wilson, "The Spade Confirms the Bible," *New York Times,* August 22, 1926, SM1; "The Ten Commandments Vindicated," *New York Times,* October 25, 1907, 10; "Was God's Voice Heard? Scholar Seeks Answer," *Chicago Daily Tribune,* October 7, 1956, C8.

9. "Recent Contributions to Archaeology," *Methodist Review* 16, no. 1 (January 1900): 140; P. W. Wilson, "The Spade Confirms the Bible," *New York Times,* August 22, 1926, SM1; "Deciphers Tablets Attributed to Moses Bearing 'Original Ten Commandments,'" *New York Times,* May 6, 1924, 1; Bishop Horace M. DuBose, "Proof of Bible Story Sought," *New York Times,* April 4, 1926, X16; G. H. Richardson, "The Value of Biblical Archaeology," *Biblical World* 48, no. 1 (July–December 1916): 21, 22; DuBose, "Proof of Bible Story Sought."

10. "For a New Commandment," *New York Times,* October 25, 1909, 1; "The 'Smokeless Sin' That Menaces Society," *New York Times,* December 1, 1907, SM3.

11. "Harvey Is Rebuked for 'Souls' Speech," *New York Times,* October 26, 1922, 7; "Harvey Raises Question: 'Have Women Souls?' If So, They Need New Commandments, He Says," *New York Times,* October 24, 1922, 1; "An Elaborate Joke Goes Wrong," *New York Times,* October 27, 1922, 15.

12. "Harvey Spoofing in Denying Souls to Women, Verdict Here," *New-York Tribune,* October 25, 1922, 3.

13. "Boy Indians in Camp," *New-York Tribune,* July 12, 1908, C3; "Ten Commandments Vindicated," *New York Times,* October 25, 1907, 10; Ernest Thompson Seton, "The Natural History of the Ten Commandments," *Century* 75, no. 1 (November 1907): 24–32; Ernest Thompson Seton, *The*

Natural History of the Ten Commandments (New York: Charles Scribner's Sons, 1907), 10ff, 32, 4, 47, 22; "Ten Commandments Vindicated," *New York Times,* October 25, 1907, 10.

14. Pietro Cimini, *My Ten Commandments for Correct Voice Production* (Los Angeles, 1936), foreword and 12, 14ff; Platon Brounoff, *The Ten Commandments of Piano Practice* (self-published, 1913), introduction. See also "Pupil of Rubinstein Says He Is Refused a Hearing," *New York Times,* January 22, 1911, SM15.

15. "The Ten Commandments of Pomology," *Prairie Farmer,* August 20, 1864, 119; "Fight Communism with the Ten Commandments of Citizenship," the back cover of *Is This Tomorrow? America under Communism!* (Cathechetical Guild, Educational Society, 1947). I would like to thank my colleague, Robert Orsi, for bringing this text to my attention. "Court Writes Decalogue for Tooting Autoists; 'Use Your Head, Not Your Horn,' He Advises," *New York Times,* January 22, 1941, 23; "'Good-Will' Precepts Bar Intolerance," *New York Times,* February 13, 1938, 45; "Ten Commandments to Beauty. Program for Today at the World's Fair," *New York Times,* July 22, 1940, 15; Paul Anka, "The Teen Commandments," http://www.lyricsmania.com/the_teencommandments_lyrics_paul_anka.html. "Temple Isaiah's Five Commandments for an Enjoyable Service," 2010, Temple Isaiah, Fulton, Maryland. Yelena Luckert, director for research and learning, University of Maryland Libraries, was kind enough to bring this document to my attention. "Ten Commandments of Good Nutrition," cited in R. Mary Griffith, *Born Again Bodies: Flesh and Spirit in American Christianity* (Berkeley: University of California Press, 2004), 210.

16. Laura Schlessinger and Rabbi Stewart Vogel, *The Ten Commandments: The Significance of God's Laws in Everyday Life* (New York: Harper Perennial, 1999); David Hazony, *The Ten Commandments: How Our Most Ancient Moral Text Can Renew Modern Life* (New York: Charles Scribner's Sons, 2010); Schlessinger and Vogel, *The Ten Commandments,* 19, 318, 112, 228, 109, 318.

17. Hazony, *The Ten Commandments,* 234, 95, 43, 17.

18. Object Number 2006.0098.0655, ca. 1880–1920, is a part of the holdings of the National Museum of American History, the Smithsonian Institution, Washington, DC, and was issued by David C. Cook Publishing of Elgin, Illinois; personal exchange with Eric Jentsch, associate curator, Division of Medicine and Science, National Museum of American

History, Smithsonian, August 20, 2007; Leigh Eric Schmidt, *Consumer Rites: The Buying and Selling of American Holidays* (Princeton, NJ: Princeton University Press, 1995), 200.

19. Suffling quoted in Schmidt, *Consumer Rites*, 196.

20. So appealing was this image that it also circulated as a pocket-sized Scripture card. The Warshaw Collection of Business Americana–Religion, Archives Center, National Museum of American History, Smithsonian Institution, is home to both versions.

21. George Dana Boardman, *Moses: A Discourse Delivered in the Meeting-House of the First Baptist Church, Philadelphia, September 23, 1888* (Philadelphia: Howard Harvey Printer), 11. As Boardman would have it, Moses was as "brave as Achilles, without Achilles's petulance; heroic as Hercules, without Hercules's savagery . . . constructive as Vulcan, without Vulcan's grotesqueness." An inventory of Moses's other attributes can be found in Bruce Feiler's *America's Prophet: Moses and the American Story* (New York: William Morrow, 2009), and in Jenna Weissman Joselit, "How Moses Became an American Icon," *TNR Online*, August 28, 2007.

22. *Moses and the Ten Commandments* (New York: Dell Publishing Co., 1957). See also Dennis the Menace, *Dennis and the Bible Kids—Moses* (Waco, TX: Field Newspaper Syndicate TMR, Word Books, 1977).

23. Please note that some of the websites I consulted when conducting my research in 2010 are no longer maintained. "Moses Action Figure," http:// www.mcphee.com/shop/products/Moses-Action-Figure.html; "Moses Action Figure, $8.95," http://www.pipefittermadison.com/; "Moses Action Figure," http://www.spertusshop.org/moses-action-figure-pr-293.html; Rob Walker, "Consumed: Jesus Christ Superhero," *New York Times*, October 7, 2007, E20; Michael Crawford, "Moses Action Figure—Another Pop Culture Collectible Review," 4, http://www.mwctoys.com/REVIEW_110907a.htm; "Action Figure—Moses Bible Quest," http://www.familychristian.com/; "Action Figures Bring Biblical Heroes to Life," *Gazette (The Colorado Springs)*, February 23, 2004.

24. "Bible Quest Action Figure—Moses," http://www.deepershopping.com/ item/biblequest/bible-quest-action-figure-moses/81596. . . . ; "Moses Action Figure," http://www.mcphee.com/shop/products/Moses-Action-Figure. html; "Moses Action Figure," http://www.spertusshop.org/moses-action-figure-pr-293.html; "Moses Action Figure—Ages 3 to 99," http://www. moderntribe.com/product/moses_action_figure.

Chapter 3

1. Congregation Anshi Chesed, Trustee Minutes, May 19, 1850, Temple Emanu-El Archives, New York City; Hyman Grinstein, *The Rise of the Jewish Community of New York, 1654-1860* (Philadelphia: Jewish Publication Society, 1945), 177; "The New Synagogue, Norfolk Street—New York," *The Asmonean,* May 3, 1850, 12; "Hebrew Customs—The Feast of Pentecost— Consecration of a new [*sic*] Synagogue," *New-York Daily Tribune,* May 18, 1850, 2. Information on architect Alexander Saeltzer is hard to come by. As architectural historian Ellen Kramer puts it, extant sources are "distress- ingly scant." See Ellen Kramer, "Contemporary Descriptions of New York City and Its Public Architecture, 1850," *Journal of the Society of Architectural Historians* 27, no. 4 (1968): 264–80. See also Jeff Richman, "An Important, But Long-Forgotten Architect," *Green-Wood Blog,* February 26, 2013; "The Astor Library," *International Monthly Magazine of Literature, Science and Art,* March 1, 1851, 436. Klara Polotai, who has been researching the career of Alexander Saeltzer for some time now, has been unfailingly generous in sharing the results of her investigation.

2. "Hebrew Customs," *New-York Daily Tribune,* May 18, 1850, 2; "The New Synagogue," *The Asmonean,* May 24, 1850, 38. On the synagogue's consecra- tion, see also "News Items," *Occident and American Jewish Advocate* VIII, no. 2 (May 1850): 107. Drawings of the synagogue's exterior and interior can be found in Rachel Wischnitzer, *Synagogue Architecture in the United States: History and Interpretation* (Philadelphia: Jewish Publication Society 1955), 53–55.

3. Trustee Minutes, Congregation Anshi Chesed, December 9, 1849; Trustee Minutes, Congregation Anshi Chesed, October 13, 1850.

4. Trustee Minutes, Congregation Anshi Chesed, October 13, 1850. On Max Lilienthal, see Bruce Ruben, *Max Lilienthal: The Making of the American Rabbinate* (Detroit: Wayne State University Press, 2011).

5. Trustee Minutes, Congregation Anshi Chesed, October 27, 1850.

6. Honestus, "Innovations," *Occident and American Jewish Advocate* VIII, no. 3 (June 1850): 136–40.

7. Trustee Minutes, Congregation Anshi Chesed, November 2, 1851; Trustee Minutes, Congregation Anshi Chesed, February 8, 1852. On the vandalization of this structure, see "Congregation Anshe Slonim," in *The Synagogues of New York's Lower East Side,* ed. Gerard R. Wolfe, photogra- phy by Jo Renee Fine (New York: Washington Mews Books: A Division of New York University Press, 1978), 96–100.

8. The late Al Orensanz, executive director of the Angel Orensanz Foundation and a most gracious host, allowed me to clamber freely about the building.

9. On the fixity of the round-topped form of the Ten Commandments, see Ruth Mellinkoff, "The Round-Topped Tablets of the Law," *Journal of Jewish Art* 1 (1974): 28–43.

10. "A Jewish Newspaper in New York," *Christian Examiner and Religious Miscellany*, March 1850, 340.

11. Ibid.

12. Kate Nearpass Ogden, "California as Kingdom Come," in *Yosemite: Art of an American Icon*, ed. Amy Scott (Berkeley: University of California Press, 2006), 23; "San Francisco Jewry," *London Jewish Chronicle*, July 19, 1907, 18; "An Artist's New Studio," *San Francisco Call*, September 3, 1895, 7; "Directs Pick for List of Twelve Blue Print Men," *San Francisco Call*, August 5, 1911, 10. See also "The Mystery of the Gilded Age Architect and His Artist Brother," *Timothy Pflueger Blog*, http://www.blog.timothypflueger.com/category/albert-pississ/. I would also like to acknowledge Ava F. Kahn for sharing her unpublished paper, "Thinking Jewish in San Francisco: Landscape and Traditions, 1850-1920s," with me. An e-mail exchange, on October 6, 2008, with Professor Marc Dollinger of San Francisco State University about the history of Sherith Israel was also quite helpful, as was Joan Libman's "Beneath Its Beautiful Dome, a Beloved Synagogue Finds It Houses Rare Artistic Treasures," *San Francisco Chronicle*, March 12, 2005, E-1.

13. Steven Merritt, visiting Yosemite in 1892, coined that lovely description. Cited in Kate Nearpass Ogden, "California as Kingdom Come," 20; Nearpass Ogden, "California as Kingdom Come," 23.

14. "Temple Sherith Israel Consecrated," *San Francisco Call*, September 25, 1905, 2.

15. "Church Design Shows New Vitality as Construction of Edifices Rises to Record Volume," *New York Herald Tribune*, December 14, 1952, 1C; Will Herberg, "The Postwar Revival of the Synagogue: Does It Reflect a Religious Reawakening?," *Commentary* 9, no. 4 (April 1950): 316; Barbara Ward, "Report to Europe on America," *New York Times*, June 20, 1954, SM 7.

16. Personal exchange with Professor Alice T. Friedman of Wellesley College, May 28, 2015. She also generously shared with me her unpublished manuscript, "The Cultured Corporation: Art, Architecture and the Postwar Office Building." "New Foothill Jewish Temple to Be Dedicated," *Los Angeles*

Times, May 9, 1965, SG_B12; "Aurora Temple Dedication Set," *Chicago Daily Tribune,* December 10, 1961, W2. See also Daniel Schwartzman, "Architect Says New Chizuk Amuno Will Express Culture of Our Times," *The Jewish Times (Baltimore),* September 24, 1954, B, C. Karen Falk, curator of the Jewish Museum of Maryland, was kind enough to make this source available. On Neveh Shalom, see Gary Miranda, *Following a River: Portland's Congregation Neveh Shalom, 1869-1989* (Portland, OR: Congregation Neveh Shalom, 1989), 129; transcript of Sylvia Frankel interview with Rabbi Joshua Stampfer, Portland, Oregon, March 16, 2015; e-mail exchange with Judy Margles, director, Oregon Jewish Museum and Center for Holocaust Education, March 26, 2015; personal exchange with Professor Natan Meier, Portland State University, November 24, 2010. On Fields of the Woods, see Timothy Beal, "The World's Largest Commandments," *Roadside Religion: In Search of the Sacred, the Strange and the Substance of Faith* (Boston: Beacon Press, 2005), chap. 5. See also "World's Biggest Ten Commandments to Be Dedicated," *Washington Post,* September 2, 1951, L6. American Jews were also beguiled by the extravagance of scale. The ark at Washington Hebrew Congregation in northwest Washington, DC, took the form of two enormous Ten Commandments tablets, which were opened by remote control. Communication with Wendy Turman, deputy director, Jewish Historical Society of Greater Washington, June 5, 2015. Meanwhile, in Buffalo, the ark at Temple Beth Zion was flanked by enormous, floor-to-ceiling Ten Commandments covered with stylized Hebrew letters. See http://exploringtheburnedoverdistrict.com/temple-beth-zion-buffalo-ny/.

17. Abe Shefferman to Rabbi Albert I. Gordon, January 28, 1949, Adas Israel Congregation Archives, Jewish Historical Society of Greater Washington; Minutes of the Board of Managers of Adas Israel Congregation, January 24, 1949, 1ff, Adas Israel Congregation Archives.

18. Abe Shefferman to Rabbi Albert I. Gordon, January 28, 1949; Rabbi Albert I. Gordon to Abe Shefferman, February 2, 1949, Adas Israel Congregation Archives; Abe Shefferman to Rabbi Albert I. Gordon, February 24, 1949, Adas Israel Congregation Archives.

19. Rabbi Ben Zion Bokser to Abe Shefferman, March 31, 1949, Adas Israel Congregation Archives.

20. Stanley Rabinowitz, *The Assembly: A Century in the Life of the Adas Israel Congregation of Washington, D.C.* (Hoboken, NJ: Ktav, 1993), 411.

21. William Schack, "Artist, Architect and Building Committee Collaborate," *Commentary,* February 1956, 160.

22. Martin E. Marty, "Interfaith at Fifty—It Has Worked!," *Judaism* 27, no. 3 (Summer 1978): 342; Adam Kirsch, "Three-Part Harmony," *Tablet,* May 17, 2011, 2.

23. Will Herberg, *Protestant-Catholic-Jew: An Essay in American Religious Sociology* (1955; repr. New York: Anchor Books, 1960), 38, 37.

24. "Note by the Editor," *Occident and American Jewish Advocate* VIII, no. 3 (June 1850): 140.

Chapter 4

1. "Gotham Sees Moses First," *Los Angeles Times,* December 23, 1923, III19; "New Wonder in the Square," *New York Times,* December 26, 1923, 8; "Big Sign for the Ten Commandments," *Exhibitors Trade Review,* January 12, 1924, 13.

2. Robert E. Sherwood, "The Hollywood Zeus," *New Yorker,* November 28, 1925, 11–12; "Interesting Work for Cinema Fans," *Los Angeles Times,* December 2, 1923, III33; "Opera Glasses on the Screen," *New York Times,* December 23, 1923, X4; "Notes about the Players," *Boston Daily Globe,* March 16, 1924, 75; "Picture Plays and People," *New York Times,* October 28, 1923, X5.

3. "Costly Film Finished," *New York Times,* November 11, 1923, X5; "Cinema 'Ideas' Abundant," *Los Angeles Times,* October 13, 1922, II1; "Idea Contest Nears End," *Los Angeles Times,* October 28, 1922, II9.

4. "Step on It, Contestants!," *Los Angeles Times,* October 30, 1922, II2; "Response in Film Idea Contest Is Revelation," *Los Angeles Times,* November 12, 1922, II1; "Cinema 'Ideas' Abundant," *Los Angeles Times,* October 13, 1922, II1; "Idea Barrage Continues," *Los Angeles Times,* October 18, 1922, II9. See also "Eight Major Awards for DeMille Idea Contest: Same Idea Hit upon by Several Persons Causes Management to Multiply Prizes," *Los Angeles Times,* November 15, 1922, II1; "Task of Career Is Set. Donor of Prizes in Greatest Contest Yet Staged Accepts Challenge to Ability," *Los Angeles Times,* November 19, 1922, II8; Alma Sierks-Overholt, "DeMille Says World Religion Is Needed," *Los Angeles Times,* December 9, 1923, 18.

5. "Great Development of the Vitagraph Company," *Film Index,* January 22, 1910, 1.

6. "Moving Pictures Sermons. The Church Field Blooming," *Views and Film Index,* May 9, 1908, 8; K. S. Hoover, "Motography as an Arm of the Church," *Motography* V, no. 5 (May 1911): 84–86, esp. 84; "Moving Picture

Sermons," *Views and Film Index*, May 9, 1908, 8. On the Bible as film, see also G. Selikovitsch, "The Bible in Hollywood," *Jewish Forum* 8, no. 8 (September 1925): 400–401.

7. "The Life of Moses – Part V," *Film Index*, February 19, 1910, 8; "Activity at Vitagraph Studios," *Film Index*, August 28, 1909, 12; "Vitagraph's 'Life of Moses,'" *Film Index*, November 27, 1905, 5; "The Life of Moses – Part V," *Film Index*, February 19, 1910, 8; "The Art of the Producer," *Moving Picture World*, January 15, 1910, 49.

8. "The Reason Why Vitagraph 'Life Portrayals' Are Now Three Reels a Week," *Film Index*, February 19, 1910, 20–21. Several scenes from "The Life of Moses" can be screened at the AFI/Cromwell Collection, Print LEA-0077, Library of Congress.

9. "The Life of Moses (Vitagraph)," *Moving Picture World*, January 15, 1910, 58; "Vitagraph Notes," *Moving Picture World*, February 5, 1910, 175; "Troubles of the Moving Pictures Actor," *Film Index*, March 5, 1910, 8.

10. "Letter to the Editor: 'Religious Productions,'" *Moving Picture World*, February 26, 1910, 304.

11. "Bible Teaching by Pictures," *Film Index*, December 4, 1909, 9; "An Excellent Suggestion for Exhibitors," *Moving Picture World*, February 26, 1910, 304; "Vitagraph Notes," *Moving Picture World*, February 19, 1910, 220.

12. "A Theatre Showing Only Biblical Themes," *Motography* 1, no. 6 (December 1911): 258; "Comments on the Films – 'Life of Moses' (Number 3) Vitagraph," *Moving Picture World*, February 5, 1910, 169.

13. "Tomb Treasures of Tut-ankh-Amen beyond Reckoning. Wealth of Gold and Gems Rivals Stories of Ali Baba and Visions of Aladdin," *New York Times*, February 18, 1923, 1; "Art from Egyptian Tomb," *Literary Digest*, March 10, 1923, 28; "Customs and Manners of the Merry, Merry Pharoahs: *The Glory of the Pharoahs* by Arthur Weigall," *New York Times*, May 13, 1923, BR8; Cecil B. DeMille to Adolph Zukor, cited in *The Autobiography of Cecil B. DeMille*, ed. Donald Hayne (Englewood Cliffs, NJ: Prentice-Hall, 1959), 257.

14. "The Cheapest Photoplay," *New York Times*, December 23, 1923, VIII, 4; "The Ten Commandments Prize-Winning Theme," *Los Angeles Times*, November 19, 1922, II1; A. H. Weiler, "Random Notes about Pictures and People," *New York Times*, January 5, 1947, X5; "Taken from Life: Jeanie Macpherson Tells How She Evolved Story of the 'Ten Commandments,'" *Los Angeles Times*, February 3, 1924, C17; "Veteran DeMille Scenarist Dies," *Los Angeles Times*, August 27, 1946, A1.

15. "Taken from Life," C17; Fay King, "Ten Commandments Again Thrills Fay King," *New York Daily Mirror*, August 29, 1924, clipping found in Rod La Rocque Scrapbook, Number 1711, Clippings/Chamberlain and Lyman Brown Theatrical Agency Collection of Dramatic Scrapbooks, Billy Rose Theatre Division, New York Public Library for the Performing Arts.

16. Unidentified advertisement for a showing of *The Ten Commandments* at the George M. Cohan Theater, ca. 1923, clipping found in Nita Naldi Scrapbook, Number 1702, Clippings/Chamberlain and Lyman Brown Theatrical Agency Collection of Dramatic Scrapbooks, Billy Rose Theatre Division, New York Public Library for the Performing Arts.

17. "Photoplays," *Chicago Post*, February 13, 1924, clipping found in Rod LaRocque Scrapbook; Lawrence Reid, "The Picture of the Month," unidentified clipping in folder marked "Ten Commandments (Cinema 1923)," Billy Rose Theatre Division, New York Public Library for the Performing Arts; "Luminaries of Shadowland Project Soul of the World in Celluloid," *American Hebrew*, March 16, 1928, 644; "New Jupiter Hurling Bolts," *Los Angeles Times*, August 12, 1923, III34.

18. Arthur Roland, "The Photodrama Review," n.d., n.p., clipping found in Nita Naldi Scrapbook; "Huge Army of Extras Leave," *Los Angeles Times*, May 28, 1923, II6; "Plan Massive Production: Complete City Will Be Erected for Early Filming of DeMille's 'Ten Commandments,'" *Los Angeles Times*, April 12, 1923, II6; "Decalogue Cast Made Real Army," *Los Angeles Times*, January 17, 1924, A11; Hallett Abend, "Old Testament Ways Revived by Players," *Los Angeles Times*, June 17, 1923, 8; "Facts about the Mightiest of All Spectacles," *Ten Commandments Souvenir Journal*, n.d., 3, Billy Rose Theatre Division, New York Public Library for the Performing Arts; "The Lost City of DeMille," *Grand Street* 13, no. 1 (1994): 198–207.

19. Rita Kissin, "The Ten Commandments – The Tale of a New Exodus," *Jewish Tribune*, January 4, 1924, 25; "Imagination Is a Help in Pushing Big Pictures," *New York Times*, June 1, 1924, X2; Louella O. Parsons, "'Commandments' Is Shown on Broadway," December 22, 1923, clipping found in Nita Naldi Scrapbook; "The Ten Commandments Uses Technicolor," *Motion Picture News*, January 5, 1924, 8; "Chariots Ordered Whole," *Los Angeles Times*, August 9, 1925, 17; Parsons, "'Commandments' Is Shown on Broadway"; Glendon Allvine, "The Lure of Israel's Story," *Jewish Tribune*, April 18, 1924, 55.

20. *The Autobiography of Cecil B. DeMille*, 254; Gabe Essoe and Raymond Lee, *DeMille: The Man and His Pictures* (New York: Castle Books, 1970),

94; "DeMille Tells Harvard What Goes into Films," *New York Times,* June 5, 1927, X4.

21. "The Screen: Remarkable Spectacle," *New York Times,* December 22, 1923, 8; Robert E. Sherwood, "Motion Pictures Column," *The Herald,* December 22, 1923, clipping found in Nita Naldi Scrapbook; James R. Quirk, "Speaking of Pictures," *Photoplay* XXV, no. 4 (March 1924): 27; "Review of 'The Ten Commandments,'" *Jewish Tribune,* March 14, 1924, 65; unidentified clipping from the *Sun-Globe,* 1923, found in Nita Naldi Scrapbook.

22. "Music of the Movies," *New York Times,* December 16, 1923, X5; "Music of the Movies," *New York Times,* January 6, 1924, X5; "The Screen: The Ten Commandments," *New York Times,* December 22, 1923, 8; "Music of the Movies," *New York Times,* January 6, 1924, X5. On Reisenfeld, see, for example, "How a Cuban Boat Builder Came to Violinist's Rescue," *New York Times,* August 3, 1924, X2, and Hugo Reisenfeld, "The Advancement in Motion Picture Music," *American Hebrew,* April 3, 1925, 632.

23. *Autobiography of Cecil B. DeMille,* 252ff; Rita Kissin, "The Ten Commandments – The Tale of a New Exodus," *Jewish Tribune,* January 4, 1924, 16; *Autobiography of Cecil B. DeMille,* 253; "East Extends Roberts Rousing Welcome," *Exhibitors Trade Review,* December 15, 1923, 13. Although most, perhaps even all, of the Jewish extras hailed from Eastern Europe, some contemporary observers, in an exoticizing frame of mind, mistook them for Yemenite Jews. "Mr. DeMille instructed his agents to get several score of these primitive Yemenites to appear in the Exodus and Golden Calf scenes," reported the *New York Times.* See "Around the Film World," *New York Times,* October 5, 1924, X5.

24. Hallett Abend, "Old Testament Ways Revived by Players," *Los Angeles Times,* June 17, 1923, III1; Kissin, "The Ten Commandments – The Tale of a New Exodus," 25.

25. Kissin, "The Ten Commandments – The Tale of a New Exodus," 25.

26. Lawrence Reid, "The Picture of the Month," unidentified clipping found in folder marked "Ten Commandments (Cinema 1923)," Billy Rose Theatre Division, New York Public Library for the Performing Arts; Will Rogers quoted in Robert E. Sherwood, December 22, 1923, clipping from *The Herald,* found in Nita Naldi Scrapbook; "Around the Movie World," *New York Times,* June 1, 1924, X2.

27. Glendon Allvine, "The Lure of Israel's Story," *Jewish Tribune,* April 18, 1924, 55.

28. Full-page advertisement for "The Ten Commandments," *American Hebrew*, June 6, 1924, 167; Edwin Schallert, "DeMille's Film Thrills," *Los Angeles Times*, December 5, 1923, III; "The Shadow Stage: A Review of the New Pictures," *Photoplay* XXV, no. 3 (February 1924): 62. On the allure of the spectacular, see "The Screen: Remarkable Spectacle," *New York Times*, December 22, 1923, 8; "National Theater Holds over Big Film This Week," *Washington Post*, October 19, 1924, SO11.

29. Sherwood clipping; "Flitting Shadows," *New York Times*, December 30, 1923, X5; unidentified clipping from *The Telegram*, December 22, 1923, found in Nita Naldi Scrapbook.

30. "DeMille's Sixth Reel," *New York Times*, January 6, 1924, X5; "Story with a Moral," *Los Angeles Times*, March 9, 1924, B22; Cecil B. DeMille, "The Public Is Always Right," *Ladies' Home Journal* 44, no. 14 (September 1927): 73; "Story with a Moral," *Los Angeles Times*, March 9, 1924, B22.

31. Louella O. Parsons, " 'Commandments' Is Shown on Broadway," unidentified clipping, December 22, 1923, found in Nita Naldi Scrapbook; "The Reel Players," *Detroit Free Press*, November 21, 1923, clipping found in Nita Naldi Scrapbook; "East Extends Roberts Rousing Welcome," *Exhibitors Trade Review*, December 15, 1923, 13.

32. "Rod Has Gift That Means Success," *Wilmington Journal*, April 17, 1924, clipping found in Rod La Rocque Scrapbook; Edwin Schallert, "DeMille's Film Thrills," *Los Angeles Times*, December 5, 1923, III; Thomas B. Hanley, "Ten Commandments Cheered at the Cohan," *Telegraph*, December 22, 1923, clipping found in Nita Naldi Scrapbook.

33. Grauman's advertisement can be found in the *Los Angeles Times*, March 23, 1924, 23.

34. " 'The Truth about Cecil B. DeMille's Paramount Masterpiece,' As Told by Rabbi Samuel J. Levenson in 'The Truth,' " *American Hebrew*, April 18, 1924, 751; "The Ten Commandments after 2448 Years," *American Hebrew*, February 1, 1924, 348; "In the Year of *Tof Raish Pay Daled*," *Jewish Daily Forward*, September 28, 1924, 25; "Made to Order for Israel," *Jewish Tribune*, January 18, 1924, 11.

35. Robert S. Bichard briefly raises that possibility in his account, *Cecil B. DeMille's Hollywood* (Lexington: University Press of Kentucky, 2004), 189.

36. Full-page advertisement in the *American Hebrew*, June 6, 1924, 167.

37. Unidentified clipping, *The Telegram*, December 22, 1923, found in Nita Naldi Scrapbook; Henry MacMahon and Jeanie Macpherson, *The Ten Commandments: A Novel* (New York: Grosset and Dunlap, 1924), 77. See also Jared Gardner, "Covered Wagons and Decalogues: Paramount's Myths of Origins," *Yale Journal of Criticism* 13, no. 2 (2000): 361–89; DeMille, "The Public Is Always Right," 74.

Chapter 5

1. Gladwin Hill, "Most Colossal of All," *New York Times*, August 12, 1956, 179; Leo Mishkin, "Cecil B. DeMille Outdoes Himself," *Morning Telegraph*, November 9, 1956, 3; "Goings On about Town: Motion Pictures," *New Yorker*, January 4, 1958, 10; Lisa de Moraes, "Ten Commandments: Moses Delivers Again on the Ratings," *Washington Post*, April 10, 2012.

2. Vincent Canby, "For DeMille, Moses' Egypt Was Really America," *New York Times*, March 25, 1984, H19; "Struggling with the Tenth Commandment," http://www.vittlesvamp.typepad.com/my_weblog/2004/08/struggling-w.html; "C.B. and Me on Passover," http://www.joi.org/celebrate/pesach/cb.shtml; Danny Miller, "Oh Moses, You Stubborn, Splendid, Adorable Fool!," *Huffington Post*, posted April 4, 2007, updated May 25, 2011. A number of my students have also indicated that they routinely watch the film before attending a Seder.

3. *Seder HaHagaddah Sheli*, Paramount Pictures Corporation, 1956. I would like to thank Professor Barbara Kirshenblatt-Gimblett for bringing this text to my attention and for sharing her personal copy. It is worth noting that its flyleaf contained a Hebrew inscription in which a set of grandparents, quoting from the biblical passage in which Moses blesses his people, gave this Haggadah as a gift to their grandson.

4. Paul Mandell, "Behold His Mighty Hand," Part Two, *Cinemagic* 32 (Winter 1985): 39; Bosley Crowther, "Lesson for Today," *New York Times*, November 11, 1956, 141.

5. Seymour Korman, "Mister Hollywood," *Chicago Daily Tribune*, August 12, 1956, F30. See also "Mount Sinai to Main Street," *Time*, November 19, 1956, 82.

6. "Epic 'Ten Commandments' Film Run Begins November 9," *American Examiner*, November 1, 1956, 10; "Cinema," *Time*, November 12, 1956, 120; "The Law by Which Men Live . . .," *The Ten Commandments Souvenir Journal*, Paramount Pictures Corporation, 1956, 1; Bosley Crowther,

"Lesson for Today," *New York Times*, November 11, 1956, 141; "Epic 'Ten Commandments' Film Run Begins November 9," *American Examiner*, November 1, 1956, 10; DeMille quoted in George C. Pratt, "Forty-Five Years of Picture-Making: An Interview with Cecil B. DeMille," *Film History* 3, no. 2 (1989): 140.

7. Steven R. Weisman, "Splendid, Stubborn, Adorable Moses Returns," *New York Times*, April 7, 1988, A26; Henry Wilcoxon with K. Orrison, *Lionheart in Hollywood: The Autobiography of Henry Wilcoxon* (Metuchen, NJ: Scarecrow Press, 1991), 226–29, esp. 228.

8. "The Ten Commandments," *Variety*, March 13, 1956, n.p., clipping found in folder marked "Ten Commandments (C. 1956)," Billy Rose Theatre Division, New York Public Library for the Performing Arts; Gladwin Hill, "Most Colossal of All," *New York Times*, August 12, 1956, 179; John McCarter, "The Current Cinema," *New Yorker*, November 17, 1956, 101; unidentified clipping, *Film Daily*, ca. 1956, found in folder marked "Ten Commandments (C. 1956)," Billy Rose Theatre Division, New York Public Library for the Performing Arts.

9. DeMille was fond of using this phrase when referring to Moses, the foundling. He referred to it most publicly in the trailer to the 1956 film.

10. James Fenlon Finley, C.S.P., "Film and Television: The Ten Commandments," *Catholic World* 184, no. 6101 (December 1956): 220; "Cinema," *Time*, November 12, 1956, 121.

11. William K. Zinsser, "Cecil B. DeMille on a Tall Ladder," *New York Herald Tribune*, November 3, 1957, D1; *The Ten Commandments Souvenir Journal*, Paramount Pictures Corporation, 1956, 21; "Address by Mr. DeMille at a Luncheon in His Honor Prior to the New York Opening of the 'Ten Commandments,' November 1956," in *The Ten Commandments Souvenir Journal*, Paramount Pictures Corporation, 1956, 2.

12. Bosley Crowther, "Screen: The Ten Commandments," *New York Times*, November 9, 1956, 35; Paul Mandell, "Behold His Mighty Hand," Part Two, *Cinemagic* 32 (Winter 1985): 33; "Cinema," *Time*, November 12, 1956, 121; Ransome Sutton, "What's New in Science: Music from Invisible Strings," *Los Angeles Times*, June 11, 1933, I15; "Cecil B. DeMille Sales Speech on Stage 17/Paramount Pictures," December 9, 1954, Garabedian Collection, Sound Recordings, Library of Congress.

13. "Goings On about Town: Motion Pictures," *New Yorker*, January 4, 1958, 10; Edwin Schallert, "Paramount Shows New Large-Screen Process," *Los*

Angeles Times, March 3, 1954, 4; film review of "The Ten Commandments," *New Republic,* December 10, 1956, 20. Henry Noerdlinger not only cited a Midrash Rabbah about the burning bush but also brought to bear a more naturalist explanation. He referred to a highly inflammatory bush that, when ignited, bursts into flames without really damaging itself. See Henry S. Noerdlinger, *Moses and Egypt: The Documentation to the Motion Picture, "The Ten Commandments"* (Los Angeles: University of Southern California Press, 1956), 23–24.

14. Aeneas MacKenzie, "Search for Three 'Lost Decades,'" *New York Times,* July 31, 1955, X5.

15. Noerdlinger, *Moses and Egypt,* 130, 111, 110.

16. Murray Schumach, "New Ways Sought in Film Trailers," *New York Times,* May 19, 1958, 28.

17. *The Ten Commandments Souvenir Journal,* Paramount Pictures Corporation, 1956, 28. See also Mrs. L. McAllister Scott, "Says 'Ten Commandments' Most Unforgettable Picture," *Atlanta Daily World,* April 30, 1957, 2; Noerdlinger, *Moses and Egypt,* 110, 142; Bob Thomas, "Biblical 'Commandments' Epic Planned by DeMille for 1953," *Washington Post,* October 29, 1952, 35.

18. Dilys Powell, "The Long, Long Trail," *London Times,* December 1, 1957, clipping found in folder marked "Ten Commandments (C.1956)," Billy Rose Theatre Division, New York Public Library for the Performing Arts; Noerdlinger, *Moses and Egypt,* 3. On Friberg, see "Arnold Friberg," *The Ten Commandments Souvenir Journal,* Paramount Pictures Corporation, 1956, 28; Edwin Schallert, "DeMille Secures Noted Artist for Film," *Los Angeles Times,* December 23, 1953, 13, and Paul C. Gutjahr, *The Book of Mormon: A Biography* (Princeton, NJ: Princeton University Press, 2012), 166–71.

19. *Ten Commandments Souvenir Journal,* 28; "Cecil B. DeMille Speech on Egypt While Shooting 'The Ten Commandments,'" November 28, 1954, RGA 8778 PN02, Garabedian Collection, Sound Recordings, Library of Congress.

20. Gabe Essoe and Raymond Lee, *DeMille: The Man and His Pictures* (New York: Castle Books, 1970), 216; "Charlton Heston to Portray Moses," *New York Times,* February 16, 1954, 29; "Epic 'Ten Commandments' Film Run Begins November 9th," *American Examiner,* November 1, 1956, 10.

21. *Autobiography of Cecil B. DeMille,* ed. Donald Hayne (Englewood Cliffs, NJ: Prentice-Hall, 1959), 427; William K. Zinsser, "Cecil B. DeMille on a Tall Ladder," *New York Herald Tribune,* November 3, 1957, D1; John McCarter, "The Current Cinema," *New Yorker,* November 17, 1956 101.

22. David M. Stowe, "Letters to the Editor," *Christian Century,* January 2, 1957, 21; Tom F. Driver, "Hollywood in the Wilderness," *Christian Century,* November 28, 1956, 1390–31.

23. Lillian Reznick Ott, "Column," *California Jewish Voice,* November 16, 1956, 4; Henry Leonard, "Dayenu," *California Jewish Voice,* November 9, 1956, 4.

24. "Excerpts from an Address by Mr. DeMille at a Luncheon in His Honor Prior to the New York Opening of 'The Ten Commandments," *Ten Commandments Souvenir Journal,* 2.

25. "By the Way . . . with Bill Henry," *Los Angeles Times,* July 2, 1957, B1; *Autobiography of Cecil B. DeMille,* 426; Melvin Maddocks, "DeMille Tells of Biblical Film," *Christian Science Monitor,* October 16, 1956, 10; Adolph Zukor quoted in Leon Gutterman, "On Film Folk," *Jewish Exponent,* March 20, 1953, D1; "DeMille on Bible Critics," unidentified clipping found in folder marked "Ten Commandments (C. 1956)," Billy Rose Theatre Division, New York Public Library for the Performing Arts.

26. "Ten Commandments—Great Spectacle," *Jewish Advocate,* November 8, 1956, A12; DeMille cited in Aeneas MacKenzie, "Search for Three 'Lost Decades,'" *New York Times,* July 31, 1955, X5. A case in point: "Even C.B. himself couldn't improve on it," rhapsodized an advertisement for the Caesarea Golf and Beach Hotel in Israel. "There's a mammoth swimming pool for the bathing maiden scene. A golf course big enough for a major battle. A colossal banquet hall and moonlit discotheque for the victory sequence. And a cast of thousands, including sports directors, social hostesses, excellent chefs and happy guests. If you'd like to be in the picture, see your travel agent. He's directing." See "The Caesarea in Israel (Cecil B. DeMille Would Have Loved It)," *Commentary,* December 1966, 10; Bosley Crowther, "Screen: 'The Ten Commandments,'" *New York Times,* November 9, 1956, 35.

27. William R. Weaver, "The Magic DeMille Blend Still There," *Motion Picture Herald,* October 6, 1956, 20; Essoe and Lee, *DeMille: The Man and His Pictures,* 287.

28. Bosley Crowther, "Lessons for Today," *New York Times*, November 11, 1956, Section 2, 1; Weaver, "The Magic DeMille Blend Still There"; unidentified clipping from *Variety*, November 5, 1958, found in folder marked "Ten Commandments (C. 1956)," Billy Rose Theatre Division, New York Public Library for the Performing Arts; Bosley Crowther, "Screen Phenomenon: DeMille's 'Ten Commandments' Amazes the Film Industry," *New York Times*, November 10, 1957, 143; William K. Zinsser, "Cecil B. DeMille on a Tall Ladder," *New York Herald Tribune*, November 3, 1957, D1.

29. Harry Levette, "Some of Hollywood's Most Beautiful Added to Case," *Atlanta Daily World*, April 27, 1955, 3; Mrs. L. McAllister Scott, "Says 'Ten Commandments' Most Unforgettable Picture," *Atlanta Daily World*, April 30, 1957, 2.

30. "Seven Suburban Theatres to Show Ten Commandments," *Jewish Advocate*, August 15, 1957, A5; "Ten Commandments Coming to Hub's Astor Theatre," *Jewish Advocate*, October 18, 1956, 10; "Ten Commandments Still Big Draw at Astor," *Jewish Advocate*, May 9, 1957, 10; "Seven Suburban Theatres," A5; "Ten Commandments Big Hit at Tivoli Theater," *Daily Defender*, November 18, 1957, 19; "'Ten Commandments' at Ashby Theatre to Be Held Over," *Atlanta Daily World*, June 1, 1957, 3.

31. "Paper Hails 'Commandments,'" *Jewish Advocate*, April 4, 1957, B17; "Council Cites Film for Community Relations Aid," *Jewish Advocate*, November 1, 1956, 5.

32. Dilys Powell, "The Long, Long Trail," *London Times*, December 1, 1957; film review of "The Ten Commandments," *New Republic*, December 10, 1956, 20; Richard L. Coe, "'Longies' May Be Lavish—But," *Washington Post and Times Herald*, November 25, 1956, H3; Stowe, Letters to the Editor, *Christian Century*, January 2, 1957, 21; "Cinema," *Time*, November 12, 1956, 122.

33. Film review of "The Ten Commandments," *New Republic*, December 10, 1956, 20.

34. "Comments Evoked by Cecil B. DeMille's Production—Ten Commandments Display Advertisement," *New York Times*, November 4, 1956, 146; Gerald Kennedy, Letters to the Editor, *Christian Century*, January 2, 1957, 20.

35. "B'nai Brith Cites 'Dangers' for Aged," *New York Times*, February 26, 1957, 25; Melvin Maddocks, "DeMille Tells of Biblical Film," *Christian Science Monitor*, October 16, 1956, 10; "Mr. DeMille and Our Torah Fund,"

Women's League Outlook, May 1956, 13; Norma H. Goodhue, "CFWC Convention Begins Tomorrow," *Los Angeles Times,* April 22, 1957, A4; "Ex-Russian Predicts Soviet Uprising," *Washington Post and Times Herald,* April 19, 1957, C18.

36. William K. Zinsser, "Cecil B. DeMille on a Tall Ladder," *New York Herald Tribune,* November 3, 1957, D1; *Paramount Press Book and Merchandising Manual,* 1957, 1966, 4.

37. *Paramount Press Book and Merchandising Manual,* 2; Thomas M. Pryor, "Hollywood Scene," *New York Times,* August 28, 1955, X5; Jess Bravin, "When Moses' Law Runs Afoul of the US's . . .," *Wall Street Journal,* April 18, 2001, A1.

38. "Library Features Mosaic Tablets," *American Examiner,* November 1, 1956, 10; Press Release from the Brooklyn Public Library, October 19, 1956, Mayor Robert Wagner Papers, Municipal Archives of the City of New York. I would like to thank Kenneth Cobb, director of the archives and devoted steward of New York's history, for bringing this document to my attention. Henry S. Noerdlinger to Dr. Ralph Marcus, July 9, 1954, Ralph Marcus Papers, Mss. 363, Box 2, Folder 7, American Jewish Archives. See also Cecil B. DeMille to Dr. Ralph Marcus, October 22, 1955, Ralph Marcus Papers, Mss. 363, Box 2, Folder 7; Ralph Marcus, "A Note on the Script of the Ten Commandments in DeMille Production," typescript, n.d., 2, Ralph Marcus Papers, Mss. 363, Box 2, Folder 7.

39. Ralph Marcus to Henry Noerdlinger, October 26, 1955, Ralph Marcus Papers, Mss. 363, Box 2, Folder 7. In his exchange with DeMille's assistant, Marcus acknowledged having received the agreed-upon fee of fifty dollars. But he now wondered if he could be more generously compensated. "In view of the published reports about the very large budget of the production of your film, I'm sure that you will not consider the combined charge of $250 excessive," he wrote. History does not tell us whether his request was honored. On the "house" for the Ten Commandments, see A. F. Mengel to Dr. Ralph Marcus, February 1, 1955, Ralph Marcus Papers, Mss. 363, Box 2, Folder 7.

40. "Ten Commandments Original Film Tablets: Lot 613–Live Auctioneers," http://wwwliveauctioneers.com/item/102558_ten-commandments-original-film-tablets, September 13–14, 2003; "Artifact: Christie's—New York—April 20, 1999, Lot 124: The Ten Commandments."

Conclusion: Pedigree

1. "Old Egypt Transplanted," *Los Angeles Times*, October 19, 1922, III; "Preparing for Commandments' 350ᵗʰ Showing," *Los Angeles Times*, May 25, 1924, B19.

2. Mel Brooks, *History of the World, Part One* (1981); George Carlin, "The Ten Commandments, Broken Down."

3. Robert Mankoff, "What's the Takeaway on All This?," *New Yorker*, November 15, 2010, 81. This cartoon is now available for sale as a poster.

BIBLIOGRAPHIC ESSAY

In the research and writing of this book, I drew on a wide raft of primary sources, from the archival to the visual and just about everything else in between, including archaeological accounts, legal briefs, newspapers, scrapbooks, sermons, and sound recordings. As I made my way through this material, I was guided by the extant secondary literature on an equally broad array of topics that ranged from medieval iconography to the politicization of religion in modern America. The endnotes to each chapter contain the documentary details. Here, I offer an overview of the published works that I found most suggestive.

When it came to framing and developing the narrative, several recent publications were extremely helpful. Kevin Kruse's *One Nation Under God: How Corporate America Invented Christian America* (New York: Basic Books, 2015) and David Sehat's *The Myth of American Religious Freedom* (New York: Oxford University Press, 2011) provided a fresh perspective on that evergreen of topics: the complicated and often vexed relationship between church and state in modern America. Mark A. Noll's *In the Beginning Was the Word: The Bible in American Public Life, 1492-1783* (New York: Oxford University Press, 2015) and Jonathan Sheehan's *The Enlightenment Bible: Translation, Scholarship, Culture* (Princeton, NJ: Princeton University Press, 2005) encouraged me to think of the Ten Commandments as a living document. Sara Lipton's *Dark Mirror: The Medieval Origins of Anti-Jewish Iconography* (New York: Metropolitan Books, 2014) and Sally M. Promey's *Sensational Religion: Sensory Cultures in Material Practice* (New Haven: Yale University Press, 2014) sharpened my thinking about the visual dimensions of faith, while Judith Resnik and Dennis Curtis's *Representing Justice: Invention, Controversy, and Rights in City-States and Democratic Courtrooms* (New Haven: Yale University Press, 2011) demonstrated just how enriching a visual approach to the law might be. Jeffrey Jerome Cohen's *Stone: An Ecology of the Inhuman* (Minneapolis: University of Minnesota Press, 2015) alerted me to the interpretive possibilities of rocks and minerals, granite and slate.

Chapter 1, "Species Humbug," benefited from Robert W. Alrutz's richly detailed account, "The Newark Holy Stones: The History of an Archaeological Tragedy," *Journal of Scientific Laboratories [Denison University]*, 1980, 1–72; from Robert Silverberg's compelling study of North American archaeology, *Mound Builders of Ancient America* (Greenwich, CT: New York Graphic Society, 1968); and from Zvi Ben-Dor Benite's stimulating narrative, *The Ten Lost Tribes: A World History* (New York: Oxford University Press, 2009). Paul C. Gutjahr's *The Book of Mormon: A Biography* (Princeton, NJ: Princeton University Press, 2012) was also most helpful, as was David M. Krueger's *Myths of the Rune Stone: Viking Martyrs and the Birthplace of America* (Minneapolis: University of Minnesota Press, 2015). Taken together, these works provided a context for understanding the hullabaloo over David Wyrick's discoveries. Leo Pfeffer's *Church, State, and Freedom* (Boston: Beacon Press, 1953) did much the same thing for the American Jewish Congress, contextualizing its position on First Amendment issues, especially in response to the Fraternal Order of Eagles. Christopher L. Eisgruber and Lawrence G. Sager's *Religious Freedom and the Constitution* (Cambridge, MA: Harvard University Press, 2007), when read in conjunction with Paul

Finkelman's richly detailed article "The Ten Commandments on the Courthouse Lawn and Elsewhere," *Fordham Law Review* 73, no. 4 (March 2005): 1477–520, was extremely useful in clarifying the Supreme Court's reasoning on the Ten Commandments, as were Joshua Green's insights into Judge Roy Moore, which he detailed in "Roy and His Rock," *The Atlantic* 296, no. 3 (October 2005), 70–82.

Chapter 2, "The Ultimate To-Do List," was informed by Steven M. Green's analysis of the relationship between the Decalogue and American jurisprudence, "The Fount of Everything Just and Right? The Ten Commandments as a Source of American Law," *Journal of Law and Religion* 14, no. 2 (1999–2000), 528–558, and by Ira C. Lupu and Robert W. Tuttle's "The Cross at College: Accommodation and Acknowledgment of Religion at Public Universities," *William & Mary Bill of Rights Journal* 16, no. 4 (April 2008) 939–997. Steven Waldman's *Founding Faith: Providence, Politics, and the Birth of Religious Freedom* (New York: Random House, 2008) was also most instructive. Leigh Eric Schmidt's *Consumer Rites: The Buying and Selling of American Holidays* (Princeton, NJ: Princeton University Press, 1995) enabled me to make sense of floral representations of the Ten Commandments. Bruce Feiler's richly detailed inquiry into Moses's popularity in America, *America's Prophet: Moses and the American Story* (New York: William Morrow, 2009), provided the mise-en-scene for understanding the current appeal of Moses action figures.

Chapter 3, "Good Neighbors," benefited enormously from Rachel Wischnitzer's seminal work *Synagogue Architecture in the United States: History and Interpretation* (Philadelphia: Jewish Publication Society, 1955), and from Jo Renee Fine's photographs of Lower East Side synagogues, which were published in Gerald R. Wolfe's landmark account *The Synagogues of New York's Lower East Side* (New York: Washington Mews Books, 1978). My understanding of American Jewry of the antebellum era was enhanced by Hyman Grinstein's classic work *The Rise of the Jewish Community of New York, 1654-1860* (Philadelphia Jewish Publication Society, 1947), and by Jonathan D. Sarna's wide-ranging *American Judaism: A History* (New Haven, CT: Yale University Press, 2004). *Yosemite: Art of an American Icon* (Berkeley: University of California Press, 2006), a handsome exhibition catalog edited by Amy Scott, shed much light, visual and literary, on the early twentieth-century allure of this national park. My sensitivity to postwar American Jewry's affinity for modernism was heightened by Susan G. Solomon's *Louis I. Kahn's Jewish Architecture: Mikveh Israel and the Midcentury American Synagogue* (Waltham, MA: Brandeis University Press, 2009) and Donald Albrecht's *Designing Home: Jews and Midcentury Modernism* (San Francisco: Contemporary Jewish Museum, 2014). Will Herberg's *Protestant-Catholic-Jew: An Essay in Religious Sociology* (Garden City, NY: Doubleday, 1955) continues to be essential reading for anyone interested in American cultural and religious history, as is Ruth Mellinkoff's essay "The Round-Topped Tablets of the Law," *Journal of Jewish Art* 1 (1974): 28–43, which places modern-day depictions of the Ten Commandments within the *longue duree* of history. Joseph Leo Koerner's *The Reformation of the Image* (Chicago: University of Chicago Press, 2004) stimulated my thinking as well.

Chapters 4 and 5, "Special Effects" and "Take Two," were abetted by accounts of Cecil B. DeMille and his oeuvre, including his own. *The Autobiography of Cecil B. DeMille,* ed. Donald Hayne (Englewood Cliffs, NJ: Prentice-Hall, 1959), furnished a consistently engaging and personal perspective on the filmmaker's busy career. Richard S. Birchard's *Cecil B. DeMille's Hollywood* (Lexington: University of Kentucky Press, 2004) was a most profitable read, as was Gabe Essoe and Raymond Lee's *DeMille: The Man and His Pictures* (New York: Castle Books, 1970); Charles Higham's *Cecil B. DeMille* (New York: Scribner's, 1973); Katherine Orrison's *Written in Stone: Making Cecil B. DeMille's Epic, "The Ten Commandments"* (Lanham, MD: Vestal Press, 1999); and Scott Eyman's *Empire of Dreams: The Epic Life of Cecil B. DeMille* (New

York: Simon & Schuster, 2010). *Reframing Culture: The Case of the Vitagraph Quality Films,* by William Uriccchio and Roberta E. Person (Princeton, NJ: Princeton University Press, 1993), shed a great deal of light on the production history of "The Life of Moses." Herbert Blumer's *Movies and Conduct* (New York: Macmillan, 1933) charted the impact of the movies on the American public, especially on its children, while Alfred Gell's celebrated essay "The Technology of Enchantment and the Enchantment of Technology," in *The Art of Anthropology: Essays and Diagrams/Alfred Gell,* ed. Eric Hirsch (London: Athlone Press, 1999), 159–86, underscored the magic of special effects. Henry Wilcoxon's *Lionheart in Hollywood: The Autobiography of Henry Wilcoxon* (Metuchen, NJ: Scarecrow Press, 1991) and Melani McAlister's *Epic Encounters: Culture, Media and U.S. Interests in the Middle East Since 1945* (Berkeley: University of California Press, 2001) highlighted the cultural stakes at play in the making, release, and reception of *The Ten Commandments* of 1956.

INDEX

meanings of, 24, 30; national
identity, 24, 160; numerical
model, 159; Oklahoma Supreme
Court decision, 173n28;
particularity of, 58; political
life, 33, 45; in postwar period,
94; public knowledge of, 2,
117; redefinition of, 62–63,
65; in religious instruction,
62–63; secularization of, 64;
spiritual guidance, 33; spiritual
meanings, 39; structural
elements, 85; successfully
mediated by film, 117–18; tamed
versions, 71–72; unifying force,
157; women's version, 60–61.
See also US Supreme Court.
Ten Commandments—
representation, absence of
elements in representation,
71; as affirmation of Judeo-
Christian tradition, 44–45;
as artifact, 32; backyard
monuments, 33; bronze tablet
theater souvenir, 155; charm
bracelet, 149; chromolithograph
posters, 71; compared to
Ark of the Covenant, 51–52;
controversy over monuments,
29–30, 40–43; depictions
criticized, 79–80; differences
in content and form, 36, 41–42;
earthenwork monument, 94;
external to the synagogue, 98;
form and meaning, 84–86;
forms of representation, 86;
giving of the Law scene, 113;
as heraldry, 159; iconoclasm
and, 30; ideas about depiction,

81; innovative representations
criticized, 77–82; legislation in
Kansas, 53–54; marble tablet
gifts from *Ten Commandments*
(1956), 151; material
representation and meaning,
23, 52, 58, 67–68, 71, 93, 149;
opposition to monuments, 35,
47; permanence of form, 84–85;
placement and displacement,
51; as politically toxic, 55;
politics and, 156–57; popular
representation, 67–68;
postwar depictions, 98–99;
public attitude toward, 35;
public display of, 39; rabbinic
ruling on representations,
81–82; recontextualized, 61–62;
religiously-motivated display,
50; scene set in California,
90–91; sculpted monuments,
94; special materiality of, 151;
in stained-glass, 77–78, 89;
symbolic significance, 48–49;
tablet form, 83–84, 86, 94;
tablets from *Ten Commandments*
(1956), 138; as talismans,
33–34; on tour, 51–52; Trenton
Decalogue monument, 46; in
various media, 2–3, 8. See also
US Supreme Court.
Ten Commandments (1923) film
(DeMille), 24–26; artifacts
from, 28, 52; cast and characters,
120; challenges to writing, 108;
Christian nature of, 123–24;
criticism of, 119–20; fate of
its set, 26–28; importance to
American Jews, 121; Jewish

Illustrations: